THE CO[

SILENCE IN MINISTRY

"The Silent Community"

Norma D. Neal

C000072452

No portion of this book may be reproduced in any form without the expressed written consent of the author or publisher. All rights reserved.

The Code of Silence in Ministry

©2014 by Norma D. Neal

ISBN: 978-0-9914246-5-8

Second Edition

Printed in the United States of America

2 4 6 8 10 9 7 5 3

Interior layout by: James T. Murray III

Scripture taken from the King James Version, Copyright ©1982 by Thomas Nelson, Inc. Used by permission. All rights reserved.

All rights reserved.

Published by:

Cranberry Quill Publishing, Inc.

111 Lamon Street, Suite 204, Fayetteville, North Carolina

www.cranberryquill.com

Table of Contents

Dedication

I dedicate this book in the hope of helping others in their quest to be delivered from the bondage of religiosity.

To my husband and best friend Kenny who has stood right by my side for over 42 years. Thank you for loving me unconditionally and trusting the God and His anointing on the inside of me. When you didn't understand me, or why I did the things I did, you just went along with what I believed God was saying for our family especially when we moved to North Carolina. You never gave up on me you were always pushing me to do all that God was calling me to. You supported me totally in completing this assignment and others.

To the children that God has blessed us with - Kenny Jr., the late Donald Robert, Anthony Warren, Sean, Dominick, Scott, and Herbert.

My daughter-in-law – Towana (Marylee) Continue to seek the Lord. Thank you for your forgiveness and love. I will always cherish our private discussions.

My sister, the late Barbara M. Johnson - I miss talking to her about our childhood. I will never forget the summer, just before she transitioned, we spent together laughing and crying over the things we watched our mother go through in the church. What an awesome mother we had. I will never forget our shopping trips to Pathmark and her love for "T-bone steaks." Her love and dedication to her children, especially her son's was historic. We will always celebrate her life as she, Nellie Rose, enjoys her new life with the Lord.

My dad, Elder Charles A. Wilson, Sr. - I miss you so much! Your hardy laugh will be forever engraved in my mind. We have had some rough times, but God! There were times I could not understand and asked why, but God! I am so thankful that forgiveness was an intricate part of our lives together and you will always be my hero. You left us to be with the Lord, but what a legacy you left with us, your children.

Acknowledgments

In this second edition, there are so many people I would like to give special thanks to:

International Pastor and friend, Mary Scott Brown: Thank you! Thank you for listening. Thank you for your unconditional friendship and honoring the anointing that God has placed on the inside of me. I will never forget our trip to the Bahamas. That is where God began to transition us for real!

Pastor Edythe Wilson: You are my BFF… Best Friend Forever. Your encouraging words, prayers and our talks will never be forgotten. Thank you for being there for me. I will never forget what God did for us on our trip to Sanford, North Carolina. He established the friendship and affirmed our relationship with Him. Don't forget the dentist office. (Need I say more!!)

Apostle Latwonda Slaughter: What more can I say! Words cannot express how much I appreciate you. When I had to make so many difficult decisions concerning ministry, you along with others prayed with and encouraged me to obey the voice of the Lord.

Pastor Veronica (Ronnie): Thank you!! Words cannot express how I truly feel at this moment. I praise God for all that He has entrusted in you. You are an outstanding Woman of God, wife, daughter and Pastor. I am so grateful to God that He allows you to call me Mother.

Taila (TJ): You have taught me so much in the world of graphics and design. Thank you for all that you have done, especially for the Code of Silence Ministry. Thank you for the confidence that you have displayed in me as a Woman of God. Thank you for your love and the respect you have demonstrated towards me as your godmother. I will not forget.

All of my Godchildren: Prophetess Darnell Johnson, Pastors Veronica & Alex Wilkinson, Tisha, Apostle Francesca Stubbs, Apostle Javer Stubbs Sr., Taila DuBose, Pastor Denise Offor, Pastor Elijah Offor, Pastor Gail McKenzie, Joshua McKenzie, Paulette Crawford.

To my spiritual children: Pastor Carl & Prophetess S. Robinson - Thank you for your support, love and honoring the anointing of God on the inside of me.

To Apostle J. Minor and the ATIC church family, Prophetess Paula Harris, Pastors Linwood and Yolanda Gunter and so many others: Thank you for your love and support.

Introduction

It is very disturbing to see how much of the structure of the Church of the Lord Jesus Christ has changed from where it began according to scripture. The church, according to the Book of Acts, had structure, compassion, love, and operated in the power and authority of the Holy Spirit as sent by Jesus the Christ.

What has happened to our identity? What has happened to the people of God that He has placed as shepherds and leaders to lead His people? Have we lost our way or the ways of our God in compromising our standards to obtain and gain the things of this world?

Church leaders (not all) have changed the configuration or structure of the church and made it about money, power, control and destroying the lives of parishioners. When there are people in this world who are looking for real answers to their problems, they are coming to the church for help. They are seeking to know a God who can bring relief and give them rest to their weary souls. They are not coming to be hurt, controlled, put down, told that they are nothing or witness many of the things they have experienced in the world in the church! Unfortunately, in many of our churches there seems to be no distinction between the sinful world and the church.

There is a sundry of good leaders who have integrity and who truly care for and love God's people. However, there are so many leaders who use the power of influence to mislead God's people and those of us who witness this choose a "Code of Silence", to protect those leaders who have left their first love. Soul winning is no longer at the forefront, but abuse, greed, and lies are. How do we know where to go or whom do we talk to when our hurt comes from our leaders? When I was abused by my Pastor, as you will read in chapter one, there was no one I could go to. I certainly could not tell anyone because he was the Pastor. Everyone loved and admired the pastor. I felt as if no one would believe me. I felt at one point that I was alone is this world. Many of us who are in the "inner circle" see our leaders say one thing and do another.

I am not oblivious to the fact that no one is perfect. We all have issues and flaws in our lives. According to the scriptures God used imperfect people, yet when they were filled with the Power of the Holy Spirit, there was a change. I will use one example: When Paul had his encounter with Jesus on his way to Damascus, he was never the same. When we have a real love for God and His statues and allow Him to have complete control over our lives, there must be a change.

We, the church, have allowed the devil to come in and infiltrate the church of God. We have set aside the very foundational teaching of the Word of the Lord and expect God to be accepting of this heresy. Most of us in the church have witnessed so much that is totally opposite of what God had intended for His church to be. As a pastor's daughter in growing up in the church I have seen so many hypocrites but like so many others, I maintained a "Code of Silence". There are some excerpts in this book about experiences others have shared with me from their own lives that I have permission to reveal to you. I believe without any reservations, that the Lord has allowed me to write this book to encourage others to look to Jesus as their perfect example, in every area of life. Jesus is soon to come, and I know He is tired of all the games, tricks, schemes, and lies within His church.

Again, I must reiterate that this book is not intended to discredit the church or any church leader. Much of the content in this book is very strong, yet true. I hope that this book will bring deliverance and repentance to all readers. I know this book will not be very popular with many pastors, leaders, and those who wish to continue to hide behind a code of silence. But this code is keeping people from being delivered and set free. I believe it is time to tell the truth in terms of the many injustices that remains prevalent within the church today.

God is NOT pleased with the suffering of His people from the unrighteousness of leaders in the House of God. His flocks are being scattered and are wandering like nomads. This is due to the fact that many leaders and members with the leader's spirit have become more concerned about building up empires, becoming rich, enjoying million dollar homes, operating in pride, expensive cars, and land, rather than watching over the souls of God's people. Many leaders are misrepresenting our Lord and Savior by teaching His people that rules, regulations, and duty is more important than holiness and righteousness.

God is concerned about his sheep (flock) being misled, and left to wander aimlessly.

Have we become so self-righteous and so untouchable with ourselves that we have forgotten from where God has brought us?

This book is not being written to the church member who is looking for an excuse to stop attending worship services because there are problems in the church. You will NOT find a perfect church. There are countless leaders who are still fasting, praying, teaching, and exhibiting the character and nature of our Lord and Savior Jesus Christ.

I write this as the Lord wills, because there are far too many souls that are out on the streets and will not come back into the church because of church hurt and the Enemy wants them to think that they are alone. I also write this book to the individuals who have experienced the abuse, misuse, emotional damage, and have been ostracized in the church.

I'd like to call this a preventative book. Let's prevent these things from happening to someone else. Of course those who were called by God to lead His flock will be held accountable to God for their action. It is not okay to abuse, misuse, offend and mislead God's people and expect God not to do anything. There will always be a consequence for sin. We look to them to lead us to the Lord in holiness and righteousness. Shepherds (pastors) are to feed, guide and tend to the flock with tender care. There are times when the shepherd provides loving protection for the flock. They are not abusive, catty or spiteful, controlling, vicious gossips or cruel. When you find individuals in the church who are such they are operating in their own way of thinking, and in their own way of doing things. This is why we must keep our minds and eyes on the Lord at all times.

It is so essential for us to maintain our own relationship with the Father. We must continue to pray for our leaders. We oftentimes pray amiss for them. I think it is not only important to pray that God will bless them financially, but include in your prayers that God will keep their eyes to see only what God would have them to see, and hear only what the Father would have them to hear, and obey Him. I also think that it is important that we ask God to keep them focused on souls. Ask the Father to lead them in all matters.

Although many people look to their leader for direction and strength, in today's world, God is making it so that we must look to Him, and Him only for everything we need. For years

I heard my parents and others say, "don't put your trust in man, man will fail you". The Bible warns us through several scriptures not to put your trust in man. Those who put their trust in man are in disobedience to God and are cursed. Jeremiah 17:5 (KJV) states *"Cursed be the man that trusteth in man, and maketh flesh his arm, and whose heart departeth from the LORD."*

Secondly, He (God) will never embarrass us, put us down, or reveal any private conversation we have had with him. He will never rape us, or tell us that we will never amount to anything. God always builds and edifies. Even when He chastises us, it is done with love and compassion.

I begin this book with my teenage experience living as a pastor's kid (PK). It's sad to see how many things in ministry over the years have not changed.

Media exposes all types of abuse on talk shows every day. However, many of us in the church never get the opportunity to let others know those same abuses can occur in the Christian church. The abuse I experienced as a child within my so-called "safe" home is still being done to many young children today.

Don't allow the devil trick you into thinking that all ministers and all ministries are the same. They are not. Don't take your frustrations out on the Lord. This is what the enemy would want you to do.

There are still so many things that the Lord had not allowed me to reveal to the public or anyone else. God knows why!!! I realize that many will try to poke holes in, and try to discredit this book. This really doesn't trouble me, because this is my story, God has given me instructions and Told Me To Write this Book!!!

Just know that: This book is not fictional it is fact!

The Code of Silence is now and forever BROKEN!!!

CHAPTER 1
PK's
"The secret sins of the saints"

Growing up as the *"Pastors daughter"*, I've heard various the jokes about being the pastors or preachers kid (PK). I heard that we were the worst kids on the block, and that we would go overboard no matter what we did. And to a certain extent that was true. Some of us would overdress, wear too much make-up, or drink too much, just to prove a point. To prove to my friends, that I was "just like them". I remember saying to myself that I could *"hang out"* too. I think some of us went overboard so that we couldn't hear the call of the Lord. When I became of legal age I would drink to drown out the voice in my ear saying to me "you don't belong here".

Sometimes I would do things just because. People (saints) in our church had high expectations of me and were continually watching us, judging us because we were the "pastor's kids". However, I wonder did people really know how powerful and hurtful their words were. Being so young and not really understanding everything, I thought I would just do what they expected me. I don't think that we were intentionally bad, we just saw and heard too much. Growing up in the "church", my sister, my four brothers, and I watched how many people who wore the title of pastor, evangelist, and pastor's wives, say one thing, but live another (secrets). At an early age I learned what a hypocrite really looks like. Their appearance and demeanor appeared to be "holy", but they were really wolves in sheep's clothing. One characteristic of a wolf is that they are treacherous and cruel. Growing up in the church I witnessed saints that talked about the love of Jesus, yet were mean, cruel and treacherous. I was confused as to what was right and wrong. Or was there any wrong at all.

The most difficult aspect of my life was to understand how *"a man of God"*, could preach every Sunday morning, Sunday night, attend in all the services required of our denomination, and at home maintain a nasty disposition, insult his wife, smoke (Kool menthol) cigarettes, drink a little beer, and have an incestuous relationship with his teenage daughter when his wife was at work.

Let me explain: After my brothers and sister went to bed, I was called into my parents' bedroom, or I was told to come into the bathroom when my father was taking a shower. I remember seeing this strong looking, tall chocolate brown man, who I loved so much, look at me differently. His eyes began to undress me as his hand began to go up my nightgown. As he began to rub me all over and kiss my back, he would tell me that I reminded him so much of my mother, when she was young. I did look like her, but I was slightly taller. My mind began to race. I'd think that "I read all about this in those true love story magazines, but never did I think this would happen to me". Certainly not with my father!! I found myself screaming within myself "somebody help me! Or STOP!" But nothing was coming out of my mouth. My father would never allow me to face him as I remember it. He would always make sure whatever he did to me was from the back.

I didn't have the sense that I had lost my innocence. At that time I really didn't know what innocence was. I just felt betrayed by my father. I felt that he had betrayed my love for him as a father, protector, and mentor. Although I had seen my parents say one thing and do another, that didn't bother me. I was used to it. So when the abuse began, I was in the state of shock. And as it progressed, I tried to push back all of my feelings. The numbness, shock, betrayal, hate, tears, bitterness and wonder bombarded my mind all at once. I wondered if I had done something wrong to cause my father to betray and disrespect me. Therefore the loss of innocence was not an issue to me, rather the betrayal was.

I would hate it when my mother went to work at night, because I knew that dad would call for me. There were times I would take a nap after school, and when everyone was outside, I would feel my father's touch on my skin. I could smell the soap he used after he had showered, and then he would be on top of me. I felt sick and dirty, and I wondered how he could? I wanted to tell my sister or my oldest brother, but I was afraid too. I was hoping that one of the nights that my father called me into his bedroom; my sister would wake up and find out where I was. We lived in a small three-bedroom house with thin walls. Sometimes we could hear my parent talking through the walls, so why couldn't anyone hear what was going on with me? At the age of 13, I wondered, was this rape? I didn't know. No one talked about incest. Although this was going on with others (secrets), no one talked about it. All I knew is that everything pertaining to boys was a sin according to the holiness church.

2

In those days I was told that it was a sin for young people to date, kiss, or even hold hands. I remember boys in junior high looking at me, and making remarks as to what they wanted to do to me sexually, and how they would do it. But they didn't touch me. I could control how far I would allow a person to go with me. I knew that I had a father that would protect me from them, but I wanted to know who would protect me from my father. I had no idea that I would need protection from my own father. I didn't have a choice in what my father did to me. I couldn't control him. And I couldn't stop it. I didn't know how.

We were told in the denomination growing up that we weren't allowed to drink, wear pants, wear make-up, and wear short sleeve blouses, hi-heels, open toed shoes, or earrings. We couldn't go to parties, movies, listen to "worldly" music, go bowling, play cards, or go horseback riding, yet, adultery, sexual and verbal abuse, stealing money, affairs or tricking people into giving money seemed to be okay.

I remember in high school, my secret boyfriend Louis G., wrote me a love letter. My father found it in my dresser drawer. That was our first fight! He hit me so hard I fell across the kitchen table. I couldn't get over the fact that this 6 foot, tall, muscular man was fighting with me, his daughter, about a letter. And he still preached on Sunday morning!!! How could he? I almost thought that this way of life was normal.

Please let me explain who my father was. He was a full time pastor and the district secretary of the district within the denominational church we were under. He was a very popular gospel personality and knew so many people. He trained my brothers how to play the guitar so much so that my brothers have travel around the world with many well-known gospel quartets and other musical artist. So within our household and among others, my father was very well known. He was also able to maintain a seasonal job as a brick mason for years, until the company shut down. I remember when He would give us money it was gritty and red from the red clay from making the bricks. My dad had a big hardy smile and laugh. The type of laugh that would make others laugh.

This is why the entire secret stuff, the treatment behind closed doors was so hard for me to comprehend. He was my father, hero, and pastor!!!

Those true love storybooks never taught me how to get out of my situation. There was no one to help me out. There was especially no advice on how to get out of a sexual relationship with my father, the pastor. My mother was not open at that time to talk about sexual subjects, and I was afraid of hurting her. Although my mother was not happy with her life, she always tried to make my father happy. When he was home from work, she would have a large dinner prepared, and we would have to wait until he came home from work before we could have dinner. She kept the house clean, with six children, and even ironed his underwear. My mother had a sweet, quiet spirit. She loved her children, especially her four boys. All four of my brothers were over 6 feet tall, yet they loved, honored and respected their 5 foot 5 inch mother.

Unlike most first ladies in the church who were very active, my mother was quiet and shy. She was not one to get up to preach or make speeches. She had a wonderful personality. People would love talking to her. Yet, if you tried to hurt any of her children, another person emerged. She became very strong, vocal, and had no problem loading a shotgun to defend her children. But when it came to my father, she remained silent. She often smiled through the silent pain.

One young lady told me that she thought she was the only one who had ever experienced sexual abuse it in the church. She was too ashamed to talk about it. She couldn't believe that her natural father would actually do something so unspeakable. *It would make it so easy for me, I thought, if my father were a stepfather.* I use to hear how stepparents or foster parents would abuse the children because they were detached. But my father was my biological father. How could he do what he did to me? I am his first born, his "special one". We were supposed to have that special bond that fathers have with their daughters. How wrong I was!

One of the most disturbing things that I had to deal with, when I began to date in my teen years is that I found myself looking for a man that reminded me of my father. I remembered his smell, his touch and all the things he did to me when I was a young girl. I had to be delivered from my father. My father was the first man I knew intimately. As the years went by I knew that this relationship was wrong. But I didn't know where to go, because I was instructed not to say anything to anybody (secrets).

I remember my father would let my brothers and sister go out to play and I had to stay in

4

and make sure the doors were locked so he could have sex with me, and he wouldn't get caught. It's funny how nobody ever came home during the time we were in the bathroom together. Not even to go to the bathroom. I would look out the back door or through the bathroom window during the time my father was having his way with me, at my friends, and siblings playing, and I'd be crying on the inside. If only I could tell them what was going on. If only I could get out of this hell, I thought to myself. I felt like a prisoner locked behind bars. I felt dirty and used. I would say to myself *"why God is this happening to me?"*

I hated it when my mother would leave for work and I knew the night was coming. I remember praying to God to let my father over sleep tonight. He wouldn't call me into his room or the bathroom. I remember one night just before he went to pick my mother up from work; he called me into the kitchen. He turned off the lights and began to rub up against me. My sister got up to go to the bathroom and my father stopped immediately. How happy I was. This gave me a chance to go back to bed without anything happening. I lay there in my bed that thanking God for helping me that night.

One day a boy walked me home from school, and we sat outside of our house on the steps talking. When my father came home from work and saw us, he flew into a rage. He called me inside and ultimately blackened my eye. That was the first time I had the opportunity to defend myself. I fought him as if I was Mohammad Ali. Of course I wasn't as strong as he was, but I wasn't going to act as if I was afraid of him any longer. I got some ice to stop the swelling and sat in my room waiting for my mother to come home.

When my mother came home from work that night, I ran to the front door to show her how her first-born looked. She seemed upset and asked me what happened, and **finally**, here was my opportunity to tell her everything. I was happy to explain to her that her husband hit me because he was jealous of my boyfriend. Why was he jealous? I was ready to answer the question. He was sexually abusing me!!! There, I thought. It was finally out. The secret was out in the open. All those terrible, nasty years are now finally out in the open. I did not have to remain silent any longer. I was happy to tell her that this man, her husband, my father, who is a preacher, was really a sinner, and a child abuser. I told her everything, knowing that she would put this man out!

But she didn't! She didn't. The hardest thing for me was when I told my mother, she told me it was my fault. She told me "I hope you go through the same things I am going through when you have daughters". Her response floored me.

Listen, when I came home from school one day and told my mother that my 5th Grade math teacher told me that I had a body that suggested to him that I should be home with a husband having children. My mother took action immediately and went to the school. She had me removed from the class, and I don't remember ever seeing that teacher again. So why didn't she have my father removed? Why didn't she rescue me? How could she take his side? What was I going to do?

I felt as if my mother had just opened my chest, and took my heart and lungs out of my body. I couldn't breathe, and my heart had stopped beating. As I was sent to my room, I listened as they argued that night. The argument was only because he hit me and I had a black eye.

I don't know what she said to him after the loud shouting and crying stopped. I just know the sexual abuse stopped.

My father didn't say too much to me after that night. During those years he NEVER apologized for the abuse. He seemed to have pushed the whole thing in the back of his mind. There was never any discussion about it at all. My mother just watched me when I was in the presence of my father. She made sure I was never alone with him again. He did not call for me in the middle of the night any more.

I never hugged, kissed, or showed any affection towards my father after the abuse. One thing for sure which did not change, my father still remained a pastor, district secretary, Gospel radio personality and husband. It was the secrets that my mother and I kept that allowed him to continue. It was not exposed because of his position in the community of the church.

Somehow, despite all I had been through, I knew I could go to the Lord. Something down on the inside of me made me feel secure when I talked to the Lord. I couldn't talk to my Pastor, who was my father. I couldn't go to my mother, because she blamed me. And I certainly could not go to any other pastor I had known, because in my mind they were frauds!!! God was my only hope. The Lord hadn't betrayed me. The Lord hadn't abused me. I needed Him. Somehow within myself I knew that the Lord could help me. Although I could not understand how or why this abuse was happening to me, I felt deep down in my soul, that God was able to bring me out. If it had not been for the Lord, I'd probably be in some institution. There was no one I could talk to but God. God had become everything to me. God became someone I could cry to, talk to, confide in, and really love. My siblings would never believe me as to what was happening, so I could not even talk with them. I felt disconnected from them. I think I really did not want them to know or hurt from this situation (I remained silent).

For the first time at the age of 16, I felt the presence of the Lord. It was at that time I realized that someone was listening to me, and not blaming me. He actually spoke to me. He told me that He would take care of me and protect me. I didn't have to worry about this abuse ever again. He (the Lord) would be with me always. For the first time in years I felt protected.

Somehow my true feelings for my father was not total hate, instead, I began to feel sorry for him. I took on this spirit of independence. I didn't need anybody to do anything for me. I felt that I had to protect myself from being abused again. I was constantly on the defensive when my father would speak to me. I thought if I had a job making my own money, my father wouldn't have much say about my daily affairs. He couldn't control me. He couldn't tell me what to do and when to do it. As it was, I felt that I didn't have any one but God. I became so confused as to who I was. I was felt that I was no longer his daughter but a person who had to protect my mother a little sister. Who could I talk to? I had trouble trying to distinguish what was truth from a lie. I had trouble because I heard one thing, but watched and experienced another.

It wasn't until years later, after I married, that I could sit down and have a full conversation with my father. I made sure my husband stayed in the room with me. I was able to confide in my husband as to what took place in my younger years and why I had taken on this independent spirit. I felt justified and very comfortable operating in that spirit.

CHAPTER 2
"A new spirit within me"

As I got older, of course my father could not say too much to me. Because I had obtained this new spirit (independence), I didn't let him say too much to my sister, or my mother. I felt that I had to protect them, especially my sister.

I wanted to protect my sister from my father's sexual abuse, and from the domination he held over my mother. I wanted my mother to know that she didn't have to be afraid of him, or do everything he wanted her to. I didn't want my mother to remain miserable, like all the other first ladies my mother considered friends in the church. Anytime my mother wanted to do something and my father said no to her, I would then say to her "Let's Go". Anytime my father would try to discipline my sister, I would step in. I wouldn't let him hit her or get too close to her. I would try to make sure she was never alone in the house with him. I would tell him to shut up when he was talking to her. I remember telling my sister to ignore everything he would say to her. Just listen to mom and me. One day my father tried to talk to my sister about cleaning the bedroom. I made sure I was there and told my sister to tell him to shut up, and of course she did so. When he demanded that she come down stairs so he could deal with her, I went instead. I dared him to touch her. Of course this lead to a fight, but I didn't care. He didn't get close to her. I knew I was in total rebellion. But at the time I felt justified. I never heard of the scripture honor thy mother and father. But I knew my father never read the scripture that children are a gift from God!!!

The spirit of innocence had left and I became someone else totally. This bold, independent, almost arrogant spirit was directing me. I also was operating under the influence of un-forgiveness. Every time I look at my dad, I only saw the abuse.

My mother was able to get me a job at the psychiatric hospital where she worked and I was able to help my mother purchase food and I paid rent. Therefore what my father refused to do for my mother; her children began to take on that responsibility. My brother and I worked and brought our own school clothes, and my sister helped take care of our younger brothers. That helped take the weight off my mother. My dad was busy being the pastor and taking care of his needs.

My mother would make the excuse that my father was an orphan, and never was allowed to enjoy things in life. He went from foster home to foster home. So I came to the conclusion that he was never delivered from his past. Apparently something happened to him going from home to home. There was a spirit that followed my father that he did not even recognize.

My mother and I would have cocktails together every Friday after payday, and then we would go shopping. It did not bother me to go with her to purchase her cigarettes, her liquor, and take her to see her boyfriend. I learned how to be a hypocrite.

Although I was hurt that my mother did not believe me, I reasoned in my mind that she was afraid of my father. She felt that she had nowhere to go, and no one to turn to. She said that she was raised to believe "once married, always married". My mother smiled through the silent pain for years. She never let on to how unhappy she really was. As far as I know, she never revealed her unhappiness to my siblings. If they were aware of it, we never discussed it. Therefore in my mind, I was not going to allow this to happen to me!! I was determined to make sure I lived a happy life and no one would ever control me as I perceived that my father controlled my mother.

Another man, who my mother met at work, had come into my mother's life. He made her feel like she was a woman and special. He showed her respect, and generally cared for her. I was happy for her because she was happy. This man brought her gifts, and would bring flowers to her at work. He would sit and talk to her. He would make sure that whatever she felt, she could express it. He told her that whatever she had to say was important to him. So it didn't bother me to go to church on Sunday, Wednesday, and Friday nights with my mother and then I would take her to meet her friend.

This outsider was a tall thin brown skinned man. His hair was black with specks of gray. He wore hospital whites all the time, and he loved to drink. I used to think that the hospital white clothes were all that he had. This man had some knowledge about the church, but he never gave his life to the Lord, and didn't want to. Yet he treated my mother, the first lady of the church, better than my father ever would. I watched their relationship grow closer. My sister, when she found out, was furious. But my sister really didn't know how miserable our mother really was.

One day this outsider could not take it any longer. My mother had told him of something

10

that my father said to her. He came to our house to kill my father. Of course my brothers and mother did not allow that to happen. But I wish so many times that my mother would have left with this outsider. She was so happy with him.

My mother would tell me how unhappy she was being saved. For years she did not enjoy the Lord. She didn't enjoy her salvation. She lived by man-made rules and regulations in the church. There were times she wanted to go to the movies, but because she was the "pastor's wife", she could not go. Besides the fact that we were taught that it was a sin to go. Mommy wanted to just be herself, but she couldn't. She had to pretend that she was happy, pretend that all was well in our home, she remained silent.

My mother was a pleasant, praying, and kind person. She had a great personality. She was short and chubby. She was very popular on her job, especially with the young people. My mother lived only for her children. She loved us very much, especially her four boys. And because she felt that she could not talk to her husband, she would confide in her children, especially my oldest brother. Mommy would tell me that many of her friends (first ladies in the church), were also miserable. I determined within myself I was not going to be saved, Holy Ghost filled and miserable.

She never wanted my sister and me to depend on a man to enjoy life, but she wanted us to remain in the church and depend on the Lord. When we all married and started our own families, she became sick (lung cancer) and died, in November 1985.

I often think that mommy didn't want to live with my father alone. Her main reason for living was gone, her children. However, my father, the pastor, turned evangelist began to enjoy his life. He dated more evangelists and missionaries than I knew were around. Saved or sinner, it didn't matter to him. In all this time, my father never stopped preaching the Word of the Lord!!

CHAPTER 3
My perception of the "Holiness" church

Although I stayed away from the church arena for many years, and I really did not want to have anything to do with the "church", yet there was something pulling at me. Because of what I had experienced at home, seen with my own eyes and what was told to me by my mother, I wanted nothing to do with the "Holiness" church. In my opinion the church wasn't holy, it was dirty. When I finally decided to visit after almost 10 years, I soon found out many things had not changed in the church.

There were still gossips, judgmental and emotionally disturbed (my opinion) within the church arena. Pastor kids watching their parents say one thing and doing another. Pastor kids sneaking out of the church after singing in the choir, when it is time for the "Word of the Lord" smoking, kissing, cussing and not wanting to hear what their father or mother is saying. Many times the "leaders" children would be outside mocking the mothers and other leaders is the church.

We used to talk about members just as we heard out parents talk about them. For example, I would hear so many leaders comment to their ministerial staff and the office staff; did you see so-and-so in the service? What kind of shout was that? Or sister so-and-so needed to just sit down instead of trying to sing that song. Everyone in the office would laugh. Maybe they didn't sound like some of the famous psalmist, but we the office staff, along with the leadership had a big laugh about it. I remember one sister wanted to get the pastors attention, and she got on the floor and began to crawl like a dog. We, the staff had a field day with that one for days. NO one informed us that it was a demonic spirit. We just perceived that she wanted to get the attention of the pastor and so did he!! We couldn't even look at that member the same without laughing at her. Or one of the staff members would comment about someone who tried their best to bring the message. The evangelists and assistant pastors would comment how "off" they were. Instead of making fun of these people, we should have encouraged them, and prayed for them. But when the head is out of order, the whole body is out of order!!

I personally heard pastors sharing members' personal conversations with others, and sometimes it was a big joke.

One pastor would constantly talk about one of the young ministers in the church. He would make everyone laugh because this evangelist was always "crying" as he put it, about how pastor would make room for other ministers to speak or minister and not her. Therefore each time we saw that evangelist coming to make an appointment with the pastor, we knew that she wanted to see the pastor to complain. This talk wasn't done in the privacy of their office, but many times in the kitchen, or at the dinner table. There would be a lot of gossip at the kitchen table talking about members and their problems.

I needed someone to help me, what you expected from us!! How was my perception of the church supposed to be!! Who was the example??

I remember when I was young, during revival services or holy convocations, after the choir would sing or after the pre-musical, we, the leader's kids, would leave and go outside. You would think that there was a party going on instead of church service. The girls would look for their boyfriends and the boys would find the pastor's daughter who was ready for anything. Our parents would be shouting on the inside and we would be kissing and feeling one another on the outside or in the back of the church.

I became a student counselor at a Christian school. Because of my background, when a student disappeared, I'd know where to find them. And sure enough, the kids (mostly the preachers, evangelist, prayer leaders, choir director or pastor grandchildren), would be in the alley, smoking or about to have sex.

There was really nothing for the youth of the church in that day, to do. I use to think when I was young, that my parents were too strict on me. I wasn't allowed to go to parties, or hang out with my friends, go bowling, or skating. They said that we had to show that we were different. We were the pastor's kids. But I realized that is wasn't so much being strict, but the fact that my parents were afraid that I would reveal all the abuse that was going on in our home, especially my father. I saw him say one thing and do another. Most of my friends had the same type of things going on and was told that they were being taught "discipline".

Ultimately my perception of the "church" was distorted. Although I felt an inner pulling to get to know God and have an intimate relationship with Him, I saw too much. What I saw, heard and experienced hindered me from having a relationship with God. I could not perceive that I needed to connect with God and not the people of the church. At that time in my love I did not know that God is Holy and not the people around me!!

CHAPTER 4
Injustice among the saints

According to Dictionary.com injustice has a meaning which includes "unfair actions or treatment". What remained with me more over the years was the injustice that the pastors wives and their families experienced. To me they seemed to suffer the most in ministry. A suffering that remained silent. This suffering appeared to be a lonely suffering. Many of my mother's friends knew the Word of the Lord. They continued to trust in the Lord to bring about a change in their homes. Sometimes this change would take a little time, or it would not change at all. Some of the pastor's wives felt that they had no choice but to remain in the marriage according to the Word of the Lord. Just as my mother felt she had to stay in her marriage. No matter how my father treated her, she said nothing.

People within the church not understanding or knowing about their smiling through the silent pain, perceived that the "family" was aloof, thought that we were arrogant or that we felt like we were better than everyone else. They never knew what was really going on. Therefore the members loved the leader and pushed aside the family members. Often times, they tried to push aside the family members, especially the children and feel sorry for the leader! REALLY!!!

I would often ask myself if this is what being a saved woman of God is like? Or is this the way her generation was taught? As a result of this silent suffering, a door was opened for the spirit of depression to come in. Depression doesn't travel alone. It brings a lot of baggage with it such as: insecurity (not trusting others), feeling rejected, offended most of the time, and being fearful. For some "first ladies" drinking, taking pills, smoking, overeating, and a spirit of self pity to name a few entered. With all these things (spirits) wrapped up in one person, it would cause one to become arrogant and distant. All these fears made these first ladies of the church appear hard in facial appearance, unconcerned, and unapproachable. They felt that they had no one they could confide in, sometimes not even to each other. They had their own silent community, where the neighbors did not know each other.

PK children would talk to each other and laugh at what was going on. Sometimes we would try to shrug it off as if it really didn't bother us, but you could see that we were just as miserable as our parents were. A first lady told me, one way to tell if a leader is telling the truth, or practicing what he/she is preaching, is to watch the spouse when that leader (spouse) is speaking. Their facial expressions or indifference will tell the story. Leader spouses have watched their husbands/wife, the pastor, become distant, unconcerned, and neglect the family.

During the time of my growing up, leaders demonstrated so much concern about sister-so-and-so, missionary so-and-so, and talk more with the church secretary than with his/her spouse. Even sharing in personal conversation with others makes many spouses feel that they were betrayed. In watching and listening to many of the first ladies of ministry, they weren't concerned about remaining "on top" so to speak. Many just want to live a life that is described in the Word of God. They have heard their husbands preach and teach about a good, abundant and prosperous life, yet they never experience it in their own lives. The bible teaches that the husband must give honor to their wives. *"Treat her with understanding as you live together. If you don't treat her as you should, your prayers will not be answered"* 1Peter3: 1-7(NLT)

A minister's wife in New Orleans said that when she would try to talk to her husband, she didn't want to hear the counseling tone that he used with the members of their church. She wanted her husband! She wanted to be held, listened to at least have a good conversation and not all the time about the church!

Of course there were some first ladies that position, prestige and authority means everything to them. They put up with a lot to remain on top. To gain that position they have been working so hard to get within their particular denomination. That topic is an entirely new book. But believe me; you have more hurting, disgusted, depressed, miserable first ladies in these churches than power seekers.

It took me a while to understand how or why my mother was not happy being saved and that most of her friends, who were pastor's wives, were drinking, and taking pills and miserable. My mother never said anything to anyone other than her children, because my father was "the Pastor"!!! Many of her friends in her circle just kept quiet. They were too ashamed and embarrassed. One pastor's wife in Westbury, Long Island just got up during church service and left her husband and the ministry and never returned. She called my mother and stated that she couldn't take it any longer. She told my mother she was tired of being a phony. She was tired of the lies, deception and being depressed. She knew that God had a better way of life for her and her children. She could not remain silent any longer. She could take the unfair treatment and disrespect from members, but it was another thing to receive the same treatment from her husband.

Apparently her husband allowed this spirit of disrespect for his wife and children to continue. As long as the members continued to honor him, do for him, he/she was fine.

I often wondered why leaders couldn't seem to communicate with their spouses. Every counselor I have ever heard concerning failing marriages, speak about open communication. How important it is to communicate. Open communication was not an option for my mother. My father just shut her out when the opportunity was available for them to talk. His total life was consumed with the church and church matters.

One pastor felt as though his wife was challenging his manhood. How absurd! All she wanted to do is try to find a common ground that they could begin to build on. Leaders appear to have a problem with pride and ego, especially the male ego! Well let me change that because I have found out that some female (leaders) care catty. They can be spiteful, nasty and unkind in the church. You can't tell them anything and they are always right. Some leaders rule and run the church just as they control their homes. There is no separation between the two!! Oh my, I am in trouble now!!! God had called them to be the leader, and only their God was going to direct them. Let me start another chapter.

CHAPTER 5
I was a silent witness!!

So many of these things I am about to share with you I was the silent witness too. Therefore because I was a part taker by remaining silent I had to go to God and to repent. I do not want to portray that I was not part of this silent community within the church, because I was. I saw, was part of, experienced and remained silent. I did not want to discredit, have people talk about my parents, or leader or other leaders I was associated with. I was fearful of the backlash from others, especially my family. Family and friends did not see and hear some of the things I witnessed in ministry. But I am not longer fearful!! God has given me this assignment to reveal what I have been silent to for years. The sad part of this, it that some of the same things that I have experienced and witnessed over a period of 30 years, is still happening within the church today.

Let me give you a few examples:

I remember one leader sat in his beautiful office, behind a beautiful cherry wood desk, being served juice by one of the ministers. He told his staff in a meeting that no one was going to tell him what he should or should not do in his ministry. The pastor's son was trying to explain to his father why he felt his father should not suspend an employee. The employee had taken off work to spend time with his family. The pastor did not display any compassion towards this employee at all. The pastor, during a shouting match with his son, explained that one of the main reasons he remained independent and not connected to other churches or denominations was that no one was going to have control over him. No one was going to tell him when to move, or what he should do in his ministry. The pastor went on to say that he wasn't going to have anyone tell him anything concerning his ministry. God would send many messages to this pastor.

This was petrifying to me. If the leader refused to open his heart, mind, and spirit to the Lord first, then to others, who could help him? There would not be any growth within the ministry as a whole. There would not be any growth on any level. The spiritual affects the natural.

So many times the children of this leader (administrators in the church) would go into meetings with their father to suggest changes or other ideas they had for the ministry. They would come out disappointed or crying. Their suggestions were turned down and disregarded.

Great men and women of God would come in to minister to the Body of Christ, and God would send a "Word" of warning to bring about a change and deliverance. And don't you know the leader would turn the message around so that the members are made to feel guilty and condemned.

They would suggest that the warning sent was just for the members, and not include the leaders. Isn't that astonishing? Doesn't warning come to the entire Body of Christ in that particular house?

The leader would get up and tell the congregation that because they refuse to obey the leader, God was sending a warning to them. You would have a congregation of people leaving a church worship service feeling worse than when they came into the service. They were not edified, built-up, or encouraged to live an abundant life in the Lord. This is one of the main reasons why many people today say they would never have anything to do with the church. I used to say it too!! I would say, *"Why should I come to the church to be put down and condemned for not giving all of my money?"*

Honorariums

This is a very HOT topic to many. Do not talk about the pay check; Honorariums. Let me make sure I make this very clear. The Bible is clear on providing for those who labor in the Lord. *I Corinthians 9:11 "If we have sown unto you spiritual things, is it a great thing if we shall reap your carnal things?"* There are other scriptures that support and tell us that we should support those that are labors in the Lord. I believe that it is essential to support and maintain such to all those who sow the pure and unmixed Gospel of Christ.

However, when money becomes the only reason you will come to minister, or finding out what your price will be to minister to God's people, there is a huge problem. In working in ministry for over 30 years as administrator the average honorariums will range from about $1,500.00 to as much as $5,000.00. Now a days you can pay well-known prophets/prophetess, evangelist, and apostles up to 30 to 40 thousand dollars. If those requirements are not met or cannot be met some who have been invited to minister, not all, will not grace the pulpit.

In these days and times there a full screening that takes place before the invited will confirm. There are certain requirements that must be met before the event takes place. Negotiations between administrators/secretaries can take many days. There are forms to be filled or questions before they are able to confirm the request. I get that. I understand why some things have to take place but my goodness some of them travel like Hollywood Movie Stars! They travel only in limousines, with bodyguards, and a huge staff (those who hold the bibles, handkerchiefs, and luggage). They would also have readers, and make sure someone is assigned to take care of their family members.

A well-known evangelist sent a confirmation letter saying that he would minister at our church, but certain guidelines had to be followed.

He had to receive $2,500.00 in advance, first class airline tickets for himself and his wife, first class hotel accommodations at the best hotel of his choice, and another $2,500.00 after he ministered one night. Hotel accommodations had to be provided for his musical staff, and his administrator. When he did come, his wife never showed up at the service. She was too busy in Manhattan shopping. I never did get to see how she looked (*smile*).

I remember a famous actor had given his life to the Lord, and had become an evangelist. He was invited to minister at our church. All the requirements this *actor* sent were met including his honorarium, which he received in advance. Over $1,500.00 was given to him, thousands of Flyers and posters were sent out. Newspaper and radio announcements went out all over New York announcing this actor's arrival. About 1000 extra chairs were rented anticipating the vast audience that would arrive. Extra security personnel were hired for the nights he was to minister.

A long white stretch limo was sent along with a welcoming committee to meet this person for the revival service. I don't think Jesus would have required what this out of work well-known actor was asking for. When the evangelist (*actor*) approached the area where the service was going to take place, a little early, he felt that the crowd wasn't large enough for him to preach too. He didn't even get out of the limousine. So he instructed the limousine driver to take him back to the hotel. He told the driver to inform the pastor that there weren't enough people there for him to preach, and he returned to California the next morning. This night the service was better than ever. Pastor preached, "I'm looking for God's plan not a man". The people never missed the "actor". We didn't have enough chairs for the people, and the altar wasn't large enough for the souls that gave their lives to the Lord.

My question is haven't they received the Word, and the anointing to do so FREELY. I believe that it is right that the "Priests" who take care of His Word and His house are honored and taken care of. When you read the Old Testament, and New Testament you will see how the Lord has set this principle into place. However, many have gone too far and made money their priority. Our ultimate goal is winning souls, not how much we are getting paid.

One evangelist, who was not very well known, went to minister at a small ministry. She felt that she should be treated and paid as if she was a famous actress. There was no limo waiting for her, no one at the front door to open it for her, no one to hold her bible, or even to read for her. She was given about $100.00 for the week. The ministry was very small, but it had people who loved the Lord, and were faithful members. She went into a rage and stated that she was ripped off, and that she would never return to that ministry again, because of the money she received. Believe me the Pastor never asked her back again. How ungrateful this evangelist was. There was no concern about souls or deliverance.

She thought that since she gave "A Word" to the church, and the pastor, she should have been paid for her services. How dare these people prostitute the Word of God, which is given to us freely!! I remained silent and cried!

CHAPTER 6
Respect of Persons/Abuse & Domination

I've listened to so many leaders state that they love God's people, yet their treatment of people displays something totally opposite. I watch leaders take pride in the fact that they pick up the homeless, bring them to their church and feed them. But what astonishes me is that when the homeless are brought into many of these services, they are seated in special seats in the back of the church or on display on the side somewhere so that their media ministry can take pictures of them. The homeless are pointed out in the service as to say "look at what I have done for them". Leaders bring in cameras and may call local politicians to come in to observe "the good works" they are doing.

Then they are given a meal for that Sunday, Friday night, or during holidays, and they are sent back to the streets. These people are not treated as you would treat a guest in your home, or a guest in the church who looks good.

They are not given the finest foods, seated on the front row of the church, or allowed to use gold goblets or crystal to drink out of. I've never seen a leader present a homeless group a large fruit basket.

In my years of being in ministry, I've never seen special hotel accommodations made for the homeless until proper housing can be found for them. Yet if a stranger came in, looking as if they were an evangelist, preacher, teacher, a "saint", they would be escorted to the front and treated with dignity and respect. What are we doing???

I remember a young lady came to our ministry, looking good, and having a good testimony. From the way she was dressed, she appeared to have "some money". She said that she was an evangelist from the Atlanta area. By the time she got finished testifying, the whole church was rejoicing. She sounded good.

Monday morning the highly energized evangelist was requesting to see the pastor. Right away, the pastor opened his door to her. She didn't have to wait or even make an appointment as others had to do. She was given a tour of the ministry, and introduced to all the staff. After her meeting with the pastor, I was making hotel accommodations for her, and a u-haul truck was being rented for her to get back to Atlanta.

Well, the following week she left, and half of the office equipment left with her, without the pastor's consent. She was never seen again, and the u-haul was never found. The ministry had to pay the cost of the u-haul.

When this information leaked out it was one of the homeless men ("a sinner") who somehow retrieved most of the equipment back.

There are ministries/churches that exploit those who are in prison. Camera's follow them as they enter the prisons. To say look what I am doing or it becomes a ploy for them to obtain money or grants to support their goals, whatever they are.

Again let me say that there are many upright, trustworthy, effective ministries and they are doing all they can for God's people according to scripture. There are so many great leaders who have the heart of the Father, who cry out daily for God's people. Many times they are the ones struggling. There are also many large ministries that are doing whatever they can as well, yet there are too many people who are being overlooked, put down and pushed aside because they look small, right in the House of God.

Abuse/Domination

One pastor entered the church office and immediately instructed the office manager to say, "yes pastor". When the office manager questioned the pastor, why should she just say yes, the leaders reply was, "because I am the leader in this house and I am the set person here". By this time all the other staff members had stopped what they were doing and began to watch the office manager. The office manager looked at the pastor with a very puzzled look, then looked around the office and said, "Yes pastor". When she did this, the pastor smiled, that sent a chill throughout the warm room. The pastor went on to tell everyone that they must obey those who have rule over them. Three weeks later the office manager resigned her position and left the ministry.

You will find pastors/leaders think that they have the right to dominate people's lives. They have the right to have power over homes, jobs, faithfulness, and dedication. And if you do not comply with what they want you to do, for the most part you are told to either leave the church, or made to feel guilty.

A staff member of a large ministry in New York had a death in his family. His first cousin had passed away. He wanted to attend the home going service, especially since this family member was close to him. When he told the pastor that he was going, he was told that he could not attend. He was told that the ministry needed him there. "Let the dead bury the dead" was quoted to him. Because the staff member respected his pastor as the man of God, he did not attend the home going service for the woman who raised him. The only thing that the staff member did that day was wash the pastor's clothes and clean his office.

Another friend of mine was a prayer counselor for a ministry and he wanted to take vacation with his family. So he put in a request as was required by the pastor. He was turned down because the pastor felt that it wasn't time for the minister to take vacation. This staff member had not taken vacation with his family because during the summer months when special services are taken place all ministers are required to be in place. Pastor's appreciation services, Founder's Day services, Men's Conferences, TV and Radio programs needed him to be on "duty". There were special events that took place during the year. When the young minister took his wife on a weekend vacation, he was suspended and his salary held back. Ultimately they left the ministry.

Another evangelist asked her leader if it was alright for her to take vacation and the leader told her NO!! I was right there and could have fallen out. First of all I could not believe that this evangelist was asking permission to go on vacation with her family. On the surface it appears that she did this out of respect for her leader. As the evangelist within this ministry she should have informed her leader of the dates of her vacation but not ask for permission!!

Let me say this as well, this became a huge issue with her family and they did not attend the ministry. The family began to look at the church as a cult. This leader felt and expressed that since he/she did not take vacation, no one should take vacation.

There is so much more I could tell you about the spirit of abuse, control and domination. There are so many people hurting from this spirit. We remain silent because we try to cover up for the leader. We want them to always look good. That is our "Code of Silence". We the inner circle remains a silent community within the church. There is something wrong when a leader wants to dictate you're every move, your home life, and control your fellowship/relationship you have with the Lord. **No one should have that right!!**

CHAPTER 7
The Inner Circle

Despite everything I had seen or experienced, believe it or not, I found myself working for over 30 years as a church secretary/administrator or assistant/office manager for large and small ministries. To this present day, I cannot tell you exactly how it happened. I wanted to be a successful, wealthy lawyer. I did not want to be part of any ministry. Certainly I did not want to be a church secretary! Church secretaries (in my day) had bad reputations. Not only did I find myself working as a church secretary but I found myself taking on the following positions: administrative personal assistant for several pastors, and well-known evangelists, ministry record keeper, bookkeeper, office manager, personal secretary to the pastor, administrator over the food pantry/soup kitchen, public relations assistant, administrator for inmate work release program, community liaison, Christian school counselor, prayer counselor and ministry proofreader. This does not include special assignments. You'll read more about this in the upcoming chapters. I loved where God had placed me and had learned so much. I was under a wonderful man of God who taught me so much about faith and ministry administration. But he also warned me and showed me that there is another side to ministry that most people are not aware of. I worked alongside female leaders who vehemently display how much they operate in the spirit of control. They loved controlling every aspect of the ministry along with the people within their ministry.

I saw where integrity was not the most prominent factor in the church. Falsifying documents to obtain money for projects were the norm. I remember hearing different ones say that the Lord had given them favor when a loan or grant was approved. If a loan or an account was approved based upon the false information that was put on the application, the leader would come out and begin to thank God for blessing the ministry. But it was a lie!! God would never bless a lie. If they couldn't obtain what was applied for, their conversation changed to the devil was trying to block it. In so many churches, the leader felt that if what he was trying to do was not successful, it was the devil.

Sometimes the leader would put the members on a ridiculous fast (did I just say that) because their schemes they used to obtain something they wanted were not working. They would preach and tell the congregation that the enemy was trying to block the ministry from succeeding. They would never tell the members all the lies and deception that was going on to obtain loans, property, etc.

I do not want to indicate that the enemy would not place road blocks in the way to stop great men and women of God purpose or assignment to build God's Kingdom. These awesome, honorable leaders do operate with integrity and will utilize wisdom that comes from God. Scripture (Isaiah 54:17a) informs us that "*no weapon that is formed against us, will prosper*". But you cannot convince me in any way that our Holy and Righteous God will prosper a lie and dishonesty. The enemy is the father of lies!!

We wonder why we do not experience awesome miracles happening in the church as we read about in scripture. What have we done to change some of the mighty power that came through those pioneers that has gone on to be with the Lord? We ask why members are disillusioned in the church. How is it that so much of what goes on in the world, has infiltrated the church? Isn't there suppose to be a difference between the world and the church in how we handle business and how we relate to others?? Of course we in the church should be different. Our standards must be higher than what we see in the world. Do you realize who opened the door for the enemy to come in? What have we done???

CHAPTER 8
"First ladies/First men"
of the church

My heart really goes out for and I pray for the "First Ladies" of the church. They experience so much abuse, rejection and for the most part are totally misunderstood along with being disrespected in ministry and yet they remain silent.

First ladies won't say anything to anyone to what really is going on because they don't want to dishonor, demean their husband (their pastor) to the membership in any way. Spouses are neglected, forgotten and many times looked over. Many times they are overlooked not just in the church but at home as well. If their spouse allows this spirit to operate, the same spirit would be carried down to the membership. There are many churches/ministries where the pastor receives all of the honor, respect and appreciation and the wife or husband would receive just a mere acknowledgement. *"OH GOD I'VE SEEN SO MUCH OF THIS"*.

Countless times you would see the pastor enter into the church, walking down the middle isle, or through the front door with his ministerial staff. One holding his/her bible, another carrying his/her briefcase and the nurse, with his/her handkerchiefs, while the first lady/man would slip in through the side door or the usher would show her/him to their seat. God help us!!

When I first started attending a large outreach ministry, I didn't know who the first lady was until 2 weeks attending the services. I only found out who she was because another member of the ministry was in love with the pastor and she wanted us to know who to pray against. This first lady was quiet, kind, beautiful, maintained a picturesque smile but had eyes like a hawk. If anyone had any type of discernment you could see that this first lady could see right through you. I found out in talking with her that she had the wisdom and anointing of God in her system. So when the small group of ladies would call the "first Lady" a witch, they were WRONG!!

You do know that people pray against the first ladies? People in the church want to have the first ladies removed. They just talk about the "first Man". Many talk or judge the man as being incompetent, not as anointed as or just lazy. Not having the spirit of his wife.

In many pulpits, leaders are seated in his/her special selected chair, along with the other elders or presbytery board. But why isn't the first lady/man seated right by their side? Why are they seated on the first row? Or off to the side somewhere? How is it that the armor bearers are seated closer to the leader than the spouse? And how is it ok with the leader? Some first ladies/man says that is Ok. But it is not. They are just used to being treated as second class citizens. If the leader allows this to continue, it will spread throughout the entire ministry. What you will end up with is the same spirit being carried into the homes of the members which in turn will cause separation, division and possibly divorce. This may be one reason that people divorce themselves from the church?

One couple who was just coming into the ministry had just gotten married and they were so much in love and loved the Lord. After observing and watching all that was going on, they disappeared. After approx.5 months they stopped attending services. The husband did not want the division he saw and within the ministry to affect his marriage and ultimately their relationship with the Lord. The leader began to put down her husband or opening display their disappointment of their family life to the congregation. What began to happen was that spirit began to infiltrate that ministry and separation/divorce became prominent. They now attend a ministry that is strong in taking care of the family and the importance of the family relationships according to the Word of God.

Not only is it the responsibility of the members to care for the leader, it also the leader's responsibility to see to it that their spouse is properly honored as well; especially if their spouse is right by their side in ministry. There are many armor bearers and intercessors for the leaders, but where are the armor bearers and intercessors for their spouses??

I watched my mother along with so many other first ladies in the church remain silent through their struggles and pain. They felt that they had no one they could turn to for help because of their position and not wanting to discredit their spouses. Usually the spouse would talk to their children. You would then have the children burdened with the damaged emotions of their parent and their own. This is where you may have PK (pastor kids) becoming bitter and wanting nothing to do with ministry until years later.

The secretaries of ministry knew more of what was going on in the ministry than the spouse. I remember an appreciation program was scheduled for the first lady. First of all, she had no input in terms of the speakers, or the program. She was just told to look good and that she would be ushered to her seat at a certain time. The next day when all the gifts of love (checks), were counted in the pastor's office, the secretary signed all the checks and the pastor deposited them into his personal bank account. The first lady was pleased with the flowers and the few expressions of love from members. And she was still smiling, with tears and hurt in her eyes. Her husband, the pastor, didn't present her with anything. This wonderful, beautiful, quiet (silent) first lady continued on with dignity. Her children and many members honored her and loved her because of what she displayed to others.

CHAPTER 9
"Affairs in the church among leaders?"

Every year the *"mother church"* would hold a general meeting or convocation out of state. My parents told me how leaders made sure they had their supply of cigarettes and beer for the hotel room for everyone to share. My mother would make me laugh when they returned from their trip and tell me which girlfriend other pastors would bring to the big denominational convention meeting every year. She shared with me how different the pastors would act when they were away from their congregations and away from home. How most of them would let their hair down so to speak.

One of her friends died from an overdose of pills and liquor. Of course it remained quiet because her husband was very well known through-out the denominational organization we were affiliated with. What was so horrifying was that the pastor had remarried 6 months later to one of the sisters in his church. This action of the pastor of course divided the church membership. However, the pastor kept on preaching and evangelizing.

I watched the events on social media that took place with well- known pastors and television evangelist which were found to have had affairs with other women. If the truth is really told, they weren't the only ones. They just got caught and the secret was exposed.

There was one leader who would disappear every Monday, after the tithes and offerings were counted and again on Thursday afternoon. No one knew where he was except another minister and his secretary. The minister would drive him to his girlfriend's house or the minister would pick them up from the hotel early the next morning.

A pastor in Florida was having an affair with his daughter. His daughter was so much in love with her father she would cook his dinner and take care of his every need. When the first lady decided to confront her husband and put an end to this secret, the husband (the pastor) and the daughter left. When this first lady was asked what took her so long to do or say anything her reply was *"he was the pastor"* she didn't want to seem like she was coming against the pastor. Most of all she was too ashamed.

I am sure that what I am sharing with you is just a small portion of what is really happening in our churches. How am I so sure you ask? Administrators and secretaries talk. They have to talk to someone. Not only are they silent they try to keep inside information confidential. We would see and hear so much that after a while it would begin to take a toll on you. It became very difficult for many of the "inner staff" to remain spiritual when they saw so much that was contrary to the Word of God. There are just as many adulteress affairs going on in the church as in the world. This should not be!!

After my mother transitioned, my father would share stories with me on how evangelists would call him and tell him that his dinner was prepared and his bath was waiting for him. These evangelist, missionaries and other leaders who wore beautiful church suits with matching accessories, which of course included the hat, said they were "saved, sanctified, filled with the precious Holy Ghost and that with a burning fire" were the first to open up their legs!! I am so sorry if that was too blunt. My intention is not to offend but to tell the truth of what has been and remains to go in in the church of God.

Another example: One pastor was celebrating his 40th pastoral anniversary. He and the first lady were escorted to their seats and the program began. As different ones came up to honor the pastor, a young man came up to the podium and introduced himself as the pastor's long lost son. The pastor's wife had no knowledge of this son. With tears in his eyes the pastor acknowledged that this was true, this announcement destroyed the family. The church family was in a state of shock and many left the church. The children stopped attending and participating in the ministry. This first lady divorced her husband and began a new life.

How can we as leaders inside the church bring real deliverance to those outside of the church, when we in the church need to be delivered ourselves? Isn't there a deliverance process that should take place within ourselves once we are saved before we become leaders over God's people? I have found that many of us in the church put on this mask as if all is well and it really is not.

CHAPTER 10
Homosexuality and lesbianism

I heard a well-known bishop declare that it is time for the church to come out of the closet and take a stand for what we believe just as the homosexual and lesbian have come out. For years this subject was not openly addressed in many churches. It was and still is to some a very controversial topic to speak on. Many leaders refuse to speak on it during their services for fear of "stepping on certain ones toes". Some feel that they do not want to come against this lifestyle because many of their parishioners or money givers are gay. Most leaders will not even have workshops, seminars or classes on this topic. One minister told me that some leaders will not address this topic because his choir director and/or musicians were gay. When growing up in the holiness church, I never heard of the word homosexual and lesbian. We just called them "funny people", or men with the broken wrist. This lifestyle which is contrary to the Word of God, has become prominent all over the world and you only had a very few leaders speak LOUD against it.

So many young people are confused in terms of who they are and what is and is not acceptable. Why? Not many leaders will take a stand and speak the truth about this spirit which is **_NOT_** from God. They appear to be afraid that they will lose members or have a legal battle on their hands. Leaders in the church have allowed known, active homosexuals and lesbians operate in leadership positions. A large portion of practicing homosexuals today sings in, or direct the church choir. In many churches today they are married, ordained as ministers, or the Minister of Music. I can't understand how leaders remain silent, indifferent and afraid to take a stand on this issue. I realize that were the Bible remains silent, many remain silent as well. However the Bible, by which we live is very vocal and address the issue of homosexuality and lesbianism. The references are: Leviticus 18:22; Leviticus 20:13; Romans1:26-27; I Corinthians 6:9-10 and of course read Genesis 19.

In one well-known ministry, the minister of music had several friends who were also practicing homosexuals and they loved to sing gospel. Before the church realized it, several of the choir members were homosexuals. So the spirit infiltrated the church. There were homosexuals driving ministry vehicles, working in the administrative staff, and teaching in Christian schools.

How is it that they are allowed to take on leadership positions or are in the fore-front and are not made to sit until they are taught the Word of the Lord and delivered from homosexuality or lesbianism? I don't believe that the church should close the doors to homosexuals and lesbians. They need the church more than ever. We need to show them the love of the Lord and teach them the Word of God and bring them to total deliverance. Many homosexuals and lesbians carry many self-damaging spirits. For example: suicide and self-mutilation.

One young man who is the minister of music and praise leader in the ministry, was about to be exposed as to his several homosexual affairs he was having with other young men in the ministry he was attending. So to avert the controversy, he asked an old girlfriend to marry him. Of course she was delighted. She thought if she married him, he would change. Approx. 3 months later, the wife was seeking council. After their wedding night, her husband refused to touch her again. Needless to say, she became pregnant on their first night together. She began talking to different evangelist in the ministry. One evangelist thought that was the perfect opportunity for her to express her love for this young lady. Now, not only did this young lady have to deal with a homosexual husband, but now she had to deal with a lesbian evangelist whom she trusted!

The young lady finally stopped all communication with everyone in leadership. Now, who would this young married woman go to? She was afraid to go to her pastor because her leader allowed practicing homosexuals to have major positions in the church. She believed that the pastor was a promoter of homosexuality and lesbianism.

There are traveling evangelists who thrive on young women who travel with them. All these young girls see is the excitement and glamour that goes along with traveling with a well known evangelist. These young women carry books, bibles, handkerchiefs, clothes, shoes and take all kinds of abuse just to be with these evangelists. Some of these evangelists have the gay spirit that follows them. These evangelists feel that they must have this entourage of young ladies or young men around them constantly to make them feel important, powerful and secure. One leader had his ministers help him dress and undress to the point of assisting him change his underwear. What??? One young minister who was in training ran out of the leaders office at that point and never returned.

One young minister in New York told me that he would dress and undress his pastor completely, daily, from underwear to shirt. He would wash his pastors underclothes, take his shirts and pants to the cleaners. After his pastor would take his daily shower, he would call the minister in and have the minister dress him. The minister would literally assist his pastor in putting on his undergarments. The young minister began to have feelings for the pastor. So he had to be delivered from the spirit of homosexuality. He left the ministry, but remains to fight to stay away.

Another pastor's wife carries the spirit of lesbianism. She began to talk about how much longs for the affection, the love, the touch and emotional support of her husband. She began to look for the attention, love and support from other women that she did not get from her husband. She may spend months away from home, preaching with other women evangelist friends, who would show her more compassion, love and emotional support than she got at home.

She told me, when she did come home, after one of her many trips, her husband (the pastor) would give her a sweet hug and continued doing what he was doing. He didn't make her homecoming anything special. She wanted and needed more.

When they did get together, some days later, she said that she was left feeling unfulfilled. She felt cold and pushed aside. She said that she felt the emotional detachment as a prostitute feels with one of her johns. There was no passion at all. Beside the fact that they had been married for more than 15 years and their sex life was nothing more than oral/anal sex. They never had penile/vagina sexual intercourse. Why did she stay? Because he was the pastor? She stated that she did not want anyone to know what really was going on. She was too ashamed and embarrassed. I asked her if she could talk to him at all? She said that for years she had tried to talk to him and still there was no change. He seemed disinterested and would continue to do what he liked best.

CHAPTER 11
Politics in ministry/Role models

Politics played a major role in the church world. Getting somewhere in the church had nothing to do with the level of anointing. Getting ahead in the church setting was based upon whom you knew, how much money you gave or how large your congregation was. It always amazed me how people with one or two members (so to speak) became bishops and apostles. But I soon found out that they paid the right kind of money, they knew how to get the right kind of offerings and most of all how to entertain the people.

One local pastor in Queens, New York was not promoted to the office of Bishop within his denomination because he didn't "kiss-up" so to speak to those in authority. The pastor refused to pay for his promotion.

He always stood on the notion that promotion came from the Lord. When this young pastor died, everyone wanted to then give him the recognition he deserved while he was alive.

Many times we would invite other ministries to fellowship with our church and the first question was asked was "how many members do you have?" Or who do you know? When I had to prepare a letter of invitation to an evangelist or pastor, I was told to always mention how large the ministry was or what well-known evangelist had come to minister. Therefore if one well-known evangelist or prophet had come to your ministry, this must mean we have the money to meet their honorarium. I recall an evangelist came to our church for the first time to do a week revival.

He began to expose from the pulpit some of the spirits that was operating in the church and how people were being manipulated. The very next morning my pastor had me make flight arrangements to send him home immediately. Then pastor began to call his friends to tell them not to allow this evangelist to come to their churches. He was blackballed. It is so sad that leaders sit in meetings and talk about other leaders and their ministries. It would be a good thing if the conversations were edifying and building up the ministry. But for the most part they discuss who can come to their ministry and who cannot. What are we teaching those who are coming up after us. What are we teaching the next generation? Are these leaders our role model for the future?

Role Models

T.V. stars, athletes, rap artist, movie personalities even cartoon characters have become role models for our children. It is very rare that you hear of children saying that their parents are their role models. If the parents were not the role model, someone in the church quite possibly the pastor was the role model. Our children who are TV watchers don't identify with Jesus as being their ultimate role model, much less someone within their own families. We the leaders of the church should be the role model not only within our own ministries but most of all within our homes. How can we be the example in other families (members) homes when we are not the example of our own home?

There should be something on the inside of us that bothers us when we see that our children don't want to follow in our footsteps. Shouldn't we take a good look at ourselves?? There was a time that the word "balance" was in our church vocabulary. Our lives must be balanced. We can enjoy the Lord of our salvation and enjoy our homes that He has blessed us with.

I've come to the conclusion that because the church is so unbalanced the world remains unbalanced. Because the church remains cold, and unconcerned towards the family, the world

What is the church portraying to our youth of today? God's church is **not** some weak, unbalanced, unorganized cold, uncaring organization as some may try to present it to be. The Bible teaches us to teach our children, (Dt.6:7), Train our children, (Pr.22:6), Provide for, (II Co. 12:14), to Nurture, (Eph 6:4), to Love, (Tit 2:4), our children.

There are so many leaders who are great preachers and teachers. They travel all over the world spreading the Good News of Jesus Christ and some are on TV, but no better mothers and fathers than those who don't even know the Lord. Some of these TV talk show hosts, who don't even claim to know the Lord, show more love, compassion and concern to their children than those of us who are "saints". We can't be examples or role models to our children when they see us lie, steal, gossip, mock, curse, dress like them, are selfish, and talk like them (slang).

The one area that the enemy uses to trap our children is sex. We cannot address this area if we are having sex with pastor so-n-so, deacon-so-n-so, evangelist-so-in-so or brother so-n-so. Don't fool yourself, your children know what you are doing.

There are many unmarried traveling evangelist bonding themselves with married women or men. The next thing you know the married wife or husband begin to assist on just one trip, then there is another trip, the first one was exciting. Then they get prophesied to that they are to be the evangelist traveling companion. And for many people, that's all it takes, one word from their idol.

One young lady in New York, who was young in the Lord, left her husband and children to follow an evangelist she had just met. Of course the young couple had problems, but they needed spiritual counseling and guidance. Instead of the evangelist helping them to stay together and seek the Lord, concerning their marriage, the evangelist gave the young lady "a Word for the Lord", to travel with her. The young lady left everything, including children to follow this evangelist. She thought she was doing right because the "woman of God" gave her a "word".

Another young lady in New York, who is gifted in the area of music, decided to leave her children and husband in the care of others to travel extensively in ministry. This young woman who is blessed to have a beautiful voice, outstanding in the area of praise and worship, was so driven on becoming famous and wealthy, all other priorities are non-existent. When her husband, who is an assistant pastor, began to have affairs with other women in the church, she, the soloist (psalmist), was shocked and hurt. But who opened the door for the enemy to come in? Of course the total blame cannot be on her, he had issues as well. But she surely opened a door. And the young children saw and heard all of this. Who were their role models?

CHAPTER 12
Dysfunctional families

For a short time I attended a Junior College under the direction of a particular denomination. During my stay there I had the opportunity to talked with many PKs (preachers kids), who for the most part, had a happy, wholesome, balanced home life. But there were and remains too many of us who did not. There are too many Christian homes that remain dysfunctional.

Too many leaders' children were a witness to abuse either physical or verbal which took place behind closed doors of their homes. Before ministry leaders would walk into the church doors an argument or sometimes fight would have just taken place. The children would her the cussing, fighting and then have to sit there and listen to their parent preach something totally different in the pulpit. The children learned how to keep silent about what they had experienced. They did not want to be embarrassed or expose their parent who they loved.

Some of my friends never took a family vacation, played games or even watched television with their parents. Their parents were too busy doing "ministry". The only outing they had ever attended is when the church sponsored an outing or took the youth day out. There was always a reason why the leader's family did not go on vacation. They did not even enjoy weekends away or family gatherings.

As I continued to talk with different PK's they informed me what their life schedule was: Sunday morning and afternoon worship service, Monday was rest day for their parent, Tuesday & Wednesday, prayer night and bibles study respectively, Thursday, appointments and other meetings with members or other leaders, Friday night evangelistic service and Saturday, choir rehearsal or other meetings if there was not a conference to attend. Therefore with this schedule as I listed, there left no time for the family. We were told that ministry must come first. Many leaders are fine with this type of lifestyle. One secretary in trying to help the pastor take a vacation did schedule one week off for the leader to go away. She was told to take it off because there was too much to do in ministry. Needless to say the first lady and the children were very disappointed. They needed to get away as a family.

A female pastor would publicly put down her husband during meetings with leaders and at times from across the pulpit. Because she disrespected her husband in this manner, it opened the door for others within the ministry as well as their children to do so. The children made it very obvious that their father's opinion meant nothing to them. They depended upon their mother, the pastor for everything. She made all of the decisions in the home, which was carried into her ministry as well. I think (my opinion) you can search it out, that the scripture I Timothy 5: 8 sums up a lot when it comes to family; *"But if any provide not for his own, and especially for those of his own house, he hath denied the faith, and is worse than an infidel"* (KJV). According to dictionary. com an infidel is an unbeliever/someone without religious faith. Providing for is supplying the means of support, and in every area for the family. Making sure that the family is functional as much as possible. Of course there will always be issues.

Another pastor would take his ministerial staff out to dinner or lunch at least once per month, but he would never take out his wife. However, he was supportive when the missionaries or evangelist wanted to take out the first lady.

A pastors daughter of New Jersey, told me that her mother (her pastor) informed her that, the needs of the pastor must come first in her life. Even before her husband. This daughter is torn between loyalty to her husband and her mother/pastor. She states that she loves her mother so much and feels that it's the Lord will for her to obey her mother/pastor. So naturally, there is a battle between the mother/pastor and the daughters' husband. One morning the mother (pastor) came into the daughter's home and entered their bedroom. While the daughter and her husband were in bed the pastor (the mother) instructed her daughter to get up out of the bed and open the store she (the pastor) was managing immediately.

The daughter's husband was so shocked he didn't say a word to his mother in law, (the pastor). The husband said that he didn't pursue this further, because his wife is having enough trouble being in the middle of both of them. He said that he cannot understand how his mother-in-law (the pastor), felt that she has the right to control his marriage life. When he tried to talk to her, she clearly states that she is the pastor and what she says goes.

Are you kidding me! What in the world is going on? All of this is true. You can't make this type of stuff up. These people have come and have openly expressed their feelings and did not know how to handle it. They did not know where to go because they felt that they did not have a leader they could go too.

My friends were Jehovah Witnesses and Catholics. I saw fathers home on Saturday and Sundays and working in the yard. Parents would take their children to amusement parks, play ball or take them out to the country to ride the horse. All we did was go to church or live in hell during the week.

Some families during the summer would take a vacation together. My girlfriends from high school would talk about how their parents would be there for them to help with homework, talk about sex, and watch TV together and go with them on school outings. I thought that the family should be a close unit, spending time together in love and fellowship; especially those who were in the church. I remember once when we were very young, my parents took us to JFK airport to watch the airplanes take off. It was thrilling for us. It was a trip that we never forgot. But when my father became the pastor nothing like that happened again.

I needed most of all a father I could talk to. I had this notion in my mind that a father would protect his daughter. Be the strong figure in her life. When that was taken from me girl I was robbed. I was robbed of the security and love that was intended for me to have.

My sister and I carried the spirit of independence and control. We weren't going to be treated like our mother was or other women were in the church. Which in turn made it very hard for our husbands until the spirit was identified. We had to come against it, cast it out of our lives and the lives of our children. We did not want our family to be dysfunctional in any way. It was very hard, because I truly believed that I was OK. It was a process. It didn't happen overnight!! Look at all the role models I had!! I thought it was all right to treat my husband as if he was a child. I felt it was alright for me to do anything I wanted and he had no rights what so ever. I was controlling, demanding and carried the spirit of Jezebel for years. Side note: you do know that the spirit of Jezebel has nothing to do with make-up? Among many other evil spirits she carried the spirit of control was prominent.

CHAPTER 13
Sex in the church

One afternoon during a lunch break the topic of sex came up. There were several young single ladies present along with several married evangelist. One evangelist pointed out loudly that the Bible says that *"marriage is honorable in all and the bed undefiled"* (Hebrews 13:4a – KJV). This is a true statement. Then she went on to say that anything that a man and women does is the bed is ok. She told those of us that were there that watching porn with your partner was ok. Well I hit the ceiling. I could not believe that this evangelist who travels all over the world was saying this to us and especially to these young ladies. There are so many that have come to the same conclusion that all things are permissible in the bed with your spouse.

Oral and anal sex is not ok and it carries the spirit of lesbianism and homosexuality. The bible teaches us that spirits don't travel alone. Pornography carries the spirit of fornication, adultery, incest, orgies, etc. All these spirits are not from God. And these spirits remain in many of our churches today. When a couple watches pornography and indulge in the act of love making, they are not making love to one another, but they are making love to the images they are watching or have seen on TV/movies. They begin to act or react like those they have watched. Sooner or later that spirit has captured their every thought. Everything they have watched being done, they now want to experiment with. It's a spirit and you need deliverance!! If you don't get delivered, you'll find yourselves doing things that you never thought you would do.

One pastor in New York/Long Island carried the spirit of adultery. He could not stop cheating on his wife. When he finished with one new missionary, he would pick-up another. Therefore his son, grandson and many of the church members carried the same spirit. The son went from young girl to young girl. The son's wife openly admitted that they enjoyed pornographic movies in the privacy of their home.

A pastor in North Carolina had separated from her husband and she would only let him home when she wanted to have sex and she needed money to pay her bills. She expressed that that was the only time she was interested in him, especially when he got paid. Isn't that what prostitutes do?

A son-in-law of a pastor told me that he needed clarity on sexual issues. What did the Bible say about sexual intercourse between married couples? His mother-in-law taught against oral and anal sex, yet he heard his mother-in-law tell his father-in-law exactly what she would do for him (sexually), if his father-in-law brought her the money she need to make the mortgage payment.

One very well-known pastor commented on TV, concerning oral sex and pornography. He stated that "where the bible remains silent, he chose to remain silent also." This meant to me that since the bible does not directly say that these things are a sin, it maybe all right. But did this not leave questions in the minds of millions watching this as to what is the right thing to do. It is obvious that he did not want to deal with this issue. The enemy has taken what should be a beautiful expression of scared love given and honored by God between one man and women in marriage and distorted it into something dishonorable and disgraceful. There is so many stories that I have knowledge of concerning sexual immorality in the church however I am not allowed to continue at this time.

CHAPTER 14
Money!!!!

I briefly touched on the topic of money in the church. There were many tricks and cover-ups. Often we the children knew that we would receive the benefits of being the leader's kids. How? Some of us could not wait until after worship service because we knew that we were going out to eat after. If the offering was good, we were headed to the restaurant. Some PK's would get homes, clothes and even our bills paid. One pastor called the home his son lives in the parish so that there would not be any questions from parishioners or IRS. Some of us would even get titles put to our names so that there would be no question as to why we were entitled to receive housing allowances or other benefits. Meaning, if you were an elder or evangelist in the ministry members would not question the fact that the church is taking care of their expenses.

There are many leaders who receive instruction from God in obtaining or raising funds for ministry. We should be obedient to the voice of God and give. Without question!! But you must be careful of the many tricks and schemes some use to acquire money to build their empire. I think one of the most prominent things (for lack of a better word right now) I have seen in getting money is when out of town apostles, prophets, evangelist come to a ministry. People will come from all over just to receive a "prophetic word" from a prophet. Out-of-towners draw large crowds. Many of these "special guest speakers" are saying nothing more than what the leader has been teaching in the local church, but people flock to these services. They come into town asking the people to get on line (money lines) with $100.00, $50.00 then they go down. They stand and shake the hands of those who are giving the $100.00 first. They also have a "word" for those who are giving what they are asking. They do the same for the $50.00 line and quite possibly for the $25.00 line then all of the sudden they ask everybody else who has an offering to come and put their money into the bucket. At that point is when "the word from the Lord" stops. Usually by that time the guest speaker has already counted how much money has been raised, his honorarium has been met and he/she is ready to go.

As the people would come up for a particular line, the leader would stand at the pulpit and count how much money was coming in. For example: when the $100.00 line had about 5 people, you knew that it meant you had $500.00. Sometimes the guest speaker would ask "how many people do we have" and the ushers or finance department would keep count. They were trained that way. If the evangelist knew her honorarium was $1,500, well they knew they needed more people on the $100.00 line. If they took too long, he/she would tell them that they would not be blessed, if they didn't give and give all they had. They would encourage the people to give their bill money and people would do so believing that God would bless them.

Those who were part of the inner circle would joke about how they would leave most of their money home, because they knew what was going to happen during the offering. I remember one evangelist would tell the people "I know where most of you ladies keep your purses. The Lord knows what you have and where you have it". Sometimes people would give all they had. Some would give their bus fare home and then had to beg someone to take him or her home. I remember people giving their rent money or mortgage. Then when it came time for them to pay their rent they didn't have it. When they would come to the church for help, they were turned down and told God will make a way. My question to them is, didn't God already make a way for them to make the money to pay their bills?? So, if that is true, didn't they just give their blessing away!! Please help me out!

A pastor's daughter told me that her father was a master manipulator. Before he became a pastor he was a salesman. So his salesmanship just continued on into the church. He could get any amount of money he wanted from his membership. He told them that if the church needed money he knew he could get it. All he had to do is make them feel guilty and condemned. He would use the Word of God to manipulate the people.

One pastor knew exactly who would get to come in from out of town to raise the money he needed. If he needed about $10,000.00, he knew who to call. If he needed more money, than another evangelist or prophetess who is known for bringing in $20,000.00 and more, would be called in.

Another manipulation tool was making the people feel condemned for not doing enough. Some pastors manipulate the Word of God so much, that the people were made to feel that if they don't give, they were on their way to hell. One leader made the congregation feel so bad because they could not come up with all of the funds for the leader's birthday celebration. This small congregation had just completed a week's appreciation celebration the month before; they **must** give the pastor $100.00 twice per month, and make a sacrificial offering for building fund and other special projects. This on top of what God requires in tithes and offerings. When this congregation could not raise the money at the particular time, there was a special session during a worship service to give the leader back all of his/her money that he/she spent for his/her birthday celebration.

I remember one evangelist would come and tell the people should make sure that their check is saved, sanctified and filled in the bank. How true, but don't manipulate the people to give.

One pastor in New York, spent over $35,000.00 of the tithes and offerings collected, remodeling his son's home (parish). This brought tears to my eyes. I couldn't believe it. It was hard for me to understand how this pastor was able to misuse ministry funds in this way. Can leaders see why people question their motives when they teach on giving money? People who are striving to please God and feel if they obey the leader, they are pleasing God.

The Bible is clear on the purposes of tithes and offerings, read Leviticus 27:30-34; Deuteronomy 14:22, Numbers 18:20, 21, Malachi 3:7-12. Tithes and offering are for the up-keep of the temple/church and church work. Not to build a personal empire.

One pastor began allowing the ministers to conduct the Sunday evening service. They were told that in order for them to receive a love offering they had to raise at least $1,000.00 per service. The pastor would joke about how some ministers would only raise about $200.00 when another could reach the $1,000.00 goal. There were times he would tell them, "maybe I should have the maintenance crew take up the offering". The concern was not souls. Just money!!

A minister in North Carolina had to apply for disability insurance that took about 120 days to be approved. During that waiting period her light bill and phone could not be paid. All other means of help, (one-shot-deal, social services) as suggested by her pastor, was exhausted. When the minister then went to her church for help, she was refused. The minister, whose husband had left her, went without electric and phone service for a long period of time. In her silence she would ask people to give her water to flush the toilet and wash. Thank God most days in North Carolina were sunny so that she could cook on her grill outside. The pastor felt that the minister should have received help from her son, who lived with her and watched the life of his mother. When the community that she lived in found out about her situation, it was then she received help that she needed. Her son couldn't understand why the church that his mother cleaned, gave her money too, and for the most part was on call for the pastor, did not help them.

I remember members coming to their pastor to ask for help, and the pastor would instruct the secretary to bring out the members tithing and offering report for the year. And based upon their record, it was determined if they would receive the financial help they needed. Or some pastors would turn people down for help if they were not a member of their church.

I was under the impression that we as believers were to have the nature and character of our father. The only thing that matter to Christ was their soul. He helped everyone. I realize that these day and times are different and people will try to use the church to get money. I believe that is where discernment and wisdom comes it to deal with those types of situations. However, I find that it is a huge problem when the church leader tries to exhort and trick people into giving all of their money to support their habits.

CHAPTER 15
Humiliation

I know that there are so many that have been witnesses to so much more than I can even put into one book. However, I am sharing not only my experience but others who have shared their stories with me over a period of 35 years. These people really love the Lord and have a heart for God. Many have already went home to be with the Lord keeping their frustrations and humiliation within their hearts and will forever remain silent.

We watched pastors/leaders humiliate their staff members as well as members. I remember one pastor had orchestrated a fund raiser for the church. She put people into groups. Each group she put together would have a captain. Each captain had to bring in a certain amount of money each Sunday morning when their group was called. How they raised the money was up to them.

So, every Sunday morning after the Word went forth, before the tithes and offering were collected, the pastor would call up each caption of the group to stand before the congregation. She then would ask each caption if they had reached their goal and if one or all did not, she would tell them that they could never be leaders, because they had failed. They failed the test of leadership. These captions were made to stand there in front of the membership and visitors and were embarrassed. The leader/pastor thought this was so funny and openly laughed at them.

As this went on, group captions were so worried about the being humiliated in front of the congregation they couldn't receive anything God was saying during the service. Each caption had fear on their minds. Fear of being laughed at and made to look and feel like nothing. Pretty soon they all left that particular church.

Another pastor had one particular staff member who took prayer calls all night, care for all the ministry vehicles the next day, open ministry and Christian school doors, and make daily errands for the pastor. And yet it was mandatory for him to attend all church services.

One day this staff member dozed off to sleep in the service. The pastors stopped the service and in front of approx. 500 church members and visitors, called this member out and began to scold him (the staff member) for dozing off. The young man did not defend himself as to why he was so tired. He kept quiet and said nothing. But he had been awake performing his duties for approx. 35 hours without sleep. He was humiliated as people laughed at him along with the pastor. They laughed not knowing how long he had been without sleep and wondered how he could possibly fall asleep on the pastor.

Another evangelist came to our church as a guest speaker. As part of the evangelist giving a "Word of knowledge", to one young lady, the evangelist announced that the young lady was a lesbian and that she needed to come to terms with what the enemy was doing to her. This young girl was so embarrassed, that she ran out and never returned to the church again. Thank God she did go to another ministry where she was shown love and was delivered from the spirit of lesbianism and is a powerful preacher to this day.

A pastor's son, who was 8 years old, came and told an elder of the church "I heard my mommy say that you didn't take up the offering right, you need more training". He had overheard a telephone conversation that the pastor was having with her sister. The elder of the ministry was so humiliated especially when he said this in from of other members and guest. The elder just held her head down and said nothing. She knew from previous experience with the pastor and her son that nothing would change if she spoke to the pastor about it.

A member of a large ministry in New York went into a counseling session with her pastor concerning an affair she was having with one of the ministers of the church. To her amazement the pastor used her story as an example as part of his sermon. Not only was she humiliated, hurt and astonished her unsuspecting family and the minister's family as well.

Many members have been humiliated by leadership because what they thought was a confidential conversation was made know to staff members or family members, or they have heard a portion of their conversation from the pulpit.

I've heard staff members called stupid, dumb, overweight, no good, good for nothing, having no mind of their own, and put out of the ministry by their leader/boss, in front of other staff members and parishioners. All these leaders have the sense that they are so above their staff

56

and members that they can just say and do anything to them and it is all right.

Do we as members of the church of God place our leaders on such a high pedestal that they become lord, kings, and controllers think higher of themselves than they ought too? Does embarrassing a person make one feel that they have power over people? Have the "titles" mean more to some than it ought to? Do we in the church honor these leaders more than we honor our God? Therefore, some of our leaders feel that they have the right to say and do anything without any consequences because they are the apostle, prophet, evangelist, teacher, pastor and bishop.

CHAPTER 16
I was miserable

Although my husband was not familiar with the world (*church arena*), I came from, and I didn't tell him of all I witnessed, I treated him as if he was one of those pastors or my father. I had my guard up constantly. I married him, but I didn't give him a chance. I didn't trust him. I loved him, but didn't trust him. I wouldn't allow him to be the husband he wanted to be to me. I was miserable. Because of what my father did to me, and I heard of what some of the other preachers daughters go through, I would watch my husband around our nieces, cousins or goddaughters, granddaughters and other sisters in the church.

I wouldn't let him play with our nieces or sit them on his lap. When our nieces came over to visit us, I would make sure I stayed in the room and watched every move my husband made. My sister was the same way with her daughter.

One pastor I was under told me that I should not allow my boys play with one another, because they could become homosexuals. She thought that their playing together was too intimate. OH, God, what did she tell me that for? I was already busy watching my husband. How could I keep such a watchful eye on my very active boys?

I was so busy trying to protect my-self. I became a security guard over my emotions and my husband and my children.

Every time my husband would get up to go to the bathroom, I'd jump up also, to make sure he wasn't slipping into any of the kid's room. And when he did go into their rooms just to check on them, you better bet I was there too. I was trying not to be like my mother, I wanted to make sure that I knew what was going on with my children. I was a mess and tired all of the time. I needed God to help me. And He did.

One night during my many all night walks, I cried to the Lord HELP!! I can't live like this any longer. I'm about to have a nervous break-down. Help me get over this. How can I forgive and forget all that has happened to me. Help me become a good, trusting, loving mother and wife. I heard this quiet voice say to me, *"Trust me, rest in me"*. A sense of security came over me. All of the sudden, I just went off to sleep. I slept like a new born baby. When I woke up that morning, something about my thinking had changed. I wasn't as nervous or as suspicious as I had been previously. I'm a beautiful full figured woman (*smile*), and I felt as though I had lost 50 pounds without exercise.

Not only that, my father came over to visit me. This time I didn't panic and not answer the door, because my husband wasn't home. But I opened it with a smile and had the nerve to hug him. He was just as surprised. My deep anger had disappeared. Although I had not forgotten, the sting of hurt and un-forgiveness wasn't there anymore.

That is why I love the song "What a mighty God we serve". God knew how miserable I was and He removed the misery from my spirit. Not just from my mind but from my spirit. He is an amazing God.

After God delivered me from my misery, a missionary asked me a question that floored me. She said "why should she trust and believe in God? Wasn't he a man?" All the men in her life had abused her, especially her husband. So why should she trust this man, the man named Jesus? Do you remember I said she was a missionary in the church of God? This was my opportunity to take a stand for the Lord. The Holy Spirit on the inside of me rose up like a lion and I began to witness to her. I was so proud to inform her that the Lord never abused her. He is always there to help and protect her. And for the first time I told my story of abuse by my father and how the Lord was there for me to protect me. How the Lord delivered me from the anger, hurt of being sexually, mentally abused and from misery. I wasn't crying any longer when I talked about what had happened to me. I no longer felt like I was a victim. I am a victor. I enjoyed a very good visit from by father. For the first time in many years, I felt like I was Daddy's little girl again. We talked, laughed, cried and just looked at each other. God had completely delivered me. Thank you Lord!! I a new relationship with my husband also was formed. I can enjoy him without being suspicious.

CHAPTER 17
Administration in ministry

The first few years with this particular ministry in Queens, New York, were the most exciting and knowledgeable times of my life. I was new in the Lord and wanted to know everything about Him (the Lord), to please him in every way. I was willing to do anything that pleased the Lord.

During my teen years I was an avid reader of women's magazines, and I was sure God was going to set me up just like those I've read about. I was going to be famous and be set up in a very prestigious law firm, working 9 to 6 and wearing designer suits! I loved law and politics. I wanted nothing to do with the holiness church because of my history with my dad and all that I had witnessed as a child. I certainly did not want to become part of the ministry staff.

To this day I'm not exactly sure how the Lord did it, but He did. After attending the ministry for a short period of time, the pastor asked me to be part of the staff when the office manager went on vacation. I was stunned. I could not believe that out of several hundred parishioners, the pastor would ask me. It took me one hour to get to work and I was there bright and early Monday morning. At 8:30 a.m. I stood nervously waiting for the Pastor to open the office door. Thank God none of the other staff members were there waiting with me because I could hear my knees knocking very loudly. I don't know how I got up the stairs leading to the main office.

I could hear pastor walking around the office area, praying. I kept saying to my-self, "I can't believe I'm here". Other staff members began to come in and greeted me warmly. At 9:00 a.m., I heard the key go into the large white door leading to the office. My heart stopped. "Here it is," I said to myself. Pastor had opened the door and greeted each one of us. To my surprise, Pastor had my desk set up with a phone and typewriter in this very small office. He asked me into his office to give me a brief overview of what my temporary responsibilities would be. I was only there to cover for the office manager, who went on vacation.

I remember my first assignment was to type out the vision that the Lord had given my pastor. From there I remained for 13 years. Over the years I went from temporary clerk, to receptionist to church secretary, to administrative personal assistant for several pastors, well-known evangelists, ministry accountant and assistant to the chief administrator, assistant bookkeeper, office manager, personal secretary to the pastor, administrator of the food pantry/ soup kitchen, public relations assistant, administrator for inmate work release program, community liaison, Christian school counselor, prayer counselor and ministry proofreader.

Although, in the beginning, there were other staff members over me, somehow, I began working right along-side my pastor and his family. Pastor personally trained me in specific areas of administration and I wanted to learn. I knew that the Lord would be pleased with me, if I obeyed the pastor. You could not convince me otherwise.

Most secretaries I've spoken with feel the need to protect the pastor's image. You always try to make sure they (the leader) look good, no matter how they make you look!! Sometimes we make excuses for the leaders' inability to sit and talk with members at the moment they are needed. We have to explain to others why the pastor has refused to help them or see them. This explanation must be in a way that is kind with compassion showing people that the leader is a caring person and not hurt the person's feelings. In reality we knew that some leaders will not assist anyone unless they are members or a good tithe payer. There were times that the pastor had to say no, because the Lord said no and there is nothing anyone can do about that. At that point I remain silent!!

During the last couple of years before I left New York to move to North Carolina God was bringing about change in me. I wanted a change in my life. I had become someone I never wanted to be. I was so busy in ministry (doing) I found that I had no time for anything and worst of all no time for God! When I first started working in the main office, I consulted God on everything. God kept me a few steps ahead in order to keep my leader ahead in some areas in business. God gave me daily instructions before I went to work and after the day was over.

Then as the ministry began to grow, so did my responsibilities. I worked by my leaders side almost 20 hours of the day including Sundays. I did not notice that I was dying spiritually. I didn't even notice or hear the warning signs. I was too busy in ministry. My personal relationship with my wonderful Savior was gone and I didn't even know when it left and neither did my leader!! According to my leader, I was doing just fine, because I was there by his/her side daily. As a matter of fact, I was just about to be ordained, only because I was there! I was too tired to pray, too tired to read the Word of God and too burned out to hear the voice of God.

I thought I was okay because I was told that I would be rewarded for working for the Lord. I really didn't notice what was happening to me until I started attending Bible college. The Dean of the school was my instructor. She began teaching us about the importance of spending time with the Lord. It was then that something hit me when she told the class it wasn't all about work, work, work, but this walk was about God.

It is FAITH that pleases the Lord. She also taught us about the importance of spending time with your family. How God honors marriage and we ought to spend time together. She talked about unity, love, communication and fellowship in the home. How the husband ought to honor and love his wife and the wife to honor and respect the husband. Then she showed us the scripture Exodus 4:24-26. This scripture shows where God was going to kill Moses because he had not fulfilled the covenant of circumcision of his son.

Moses was so busy doing other things that he forgot to follow God's command completely. Moses could not effectively serve as a deliverer of God's people until he had fulfilled the conditions of God's covenant.

It was after Moses wife had completed the command of God, for their family to be blessed; that God then sent Moses and Aaron to Pharaoh. Of course the Dean of the Bible school and the pastor did not agree on this scripture at all. When he learned of this teaching, there was a huge argument. Eventually the Dean was let go.

My husband tried on several occasions to tell me that I had my priorities all mixed up. But I thought all he wanted to do was control me. After all, my leader didn't feel it was necessary for me to go home early. My leader told me on more than one occasion that the ministry must come first. We had to pray for the spirit of our leader. He had the same spirit, WORK, WORK, WORK!! I never saw him spend time with his family. For the most part, he only had meetings with his family concerning ministry.

In the beginning years my salary was a token of love, and I didn't mind, (Col. 3:23, 24). The staff was taught *"...and whatsoever ye do, do it heartily, as to the lord, and not unto men; knowing that of the lord ye shall receive the reward of the inheritance; for ye serve the lord Christ"*.

I began to learn more about faith in God's Word, commitment, church government, policies, church politics and protocol. I was introduced to hundreds of other businessmen and women, well-known ministries, Christian radio personalities, famous and well-known apostles, prophets, evangelist, pastors, teachers, Christian celebrities, local and state politicians and community leaders. With all of this going for me, how in the world could I be dying spiritually, losing my relationship with the Lord and about to lose my home?

For some secretaries, it takes a little time for them to clear their head and to pray for deliverance from being insulted, put down, misunderstood, or taking the responsibility of someone else's mistake. So, whatever the Holy Spirit is trying to do for us during a service, nine times out of ten, we've missed it.

Many secretaries would never go to the pastor for fear of placing more burdens on the man or woman of God, or for fear of being made to feel guilty and told that we had to repent for complaining. Most of us are told that God placed us in the ministry to take the weight off of the pastor. One leader's words were "We must be an asset not a liability".

CHAPTER 18
The ministry was growing

As the ministry began to grow by leaps and bounds, my working hours became longer and longer. 9:00 am to 5:00pm became 7:am to 10:pm. Then 6:00 a.m. to 2:00 a.m. especially if there were special events or conferences. I began to realize how easy it was to fall into the trap that the devil has devised to keep the "people of God" occupied and not praying. More and more people were becoming members and the new members wanted to spend more time with the pastor. It seemed as though the membership went from 500 to over 2000 within a matter of 2 years. Therefore instead of the open door policy that the pastor previously had, now appointments had to be made. No longer could one just walk into the office and request to see the pastor. They had to talk with the receptionist at her desk, and then see me to make the appointments. Some of my responsibility included scheduling appointments, answer phones, taking prayer calls, assisting the bookkeeper with preparing finances for deposits, at times making deposits, documenting all tithes and offerings, proofreading all documents before the pastor received them for final approval. I assisted the pastor with all staff meetings, business meetings, leaders meetings, and personal appointments. Assisted at least 15 or more department leaders for upcoming events and kept them updated on all ministry activities. Made sure all personal mortgages were paid on time. Assisted members, who had lost family members, assisted those who had needed assistance with food, clothing and were homeless. Prepared the distribution of TV and radio broadcast tapes. I had the responsibility of taking care of pastor's travel/hotel arrangements and all special guest who were coming in. Assisted the administrative staff in the Christian School, assisted the chief assistant administrator, and trained all new staff and so much more. The other 2 secretaries had their responsibilities, which kept them equally absorbed.

Growing pains within the ministry began and the members who were "pillars of the ministry", began to have problems with many of the changes that were taking place. The pastor wasn't as accessible as he had been, and it now was the "church secretaries" as one member put it that was keeping them from seeing pastor. To avoid the secretary, members would wait in the hall for the pastor to pass by so they could "just see him/her for one minute" to begin their counseling session or wait at the edge of the pulpit for just "one minute" of his time as he/she was leaving (secretaries know what I'm talking about).

After several meetings called by the pastor, the secretarial staff now became security guards. We literally had to guard the office from members just barging in.

When we realized that pastor was almost finished in the pulpit ministering, it was our responsibility to get to the main office ahead of time. Then when pastor came into his office after service, we would guard the door from members until he finished redressing and was ready to see those he had chosen to see. Most of the personal ministers or armor bearers were too busy holding pastor's brief case/bibles or handkerchiefs! When they had finished their responsibility, they went home.

Along with all the changes within the ministry itself (church growth), many changes were taken place within my pastor. I watched his every move and moods for years. I knew when something was bothering him/her, I knew when he/she did not pray that morning, I knew when he/she did not fast as they had directed others. I knew when he didn't want to be bothered and what he expected from his staff. So when changes began to take place in his life, I knew it. He wasn't the man of faith, I had admired over the years. He was so involved in all areas of the ministry; he no longer had the time to spend with the Lord.

So as these changes began to take place, I found myself trying to help the pastor more and more, but at the same time I became too busy to make sure my relationship and fellowship with God was intact. My relationship with my husband and children began to suffer. Remember as I talked about in a previous chapter, I became too tired and busy to pray and read God's Word. Isn't it ironic that I didn't have time to spend time with the person I was working for?

I became too busy and exhausted to talk and spend time with my family. I didn't take the time for them because I was doing the Lords work. I found out for myself training other secretaries that as the "vision became plain" (Habakkuk 2:2) and the pastor looked to run with it. I found that not everyone wanted to run with the "vision". And as it began to grow, we had more responsibility. Although there were many people coming into the ministry and giving their lives to the Lord, with skill and talent our pastor only trusted a few people. Therefore, we had many,

many, many responsibilities. The administrative staff became promoters of the new vision and mediators between department leaders, acquaintances, friends, some family members, whose feelings are now hurt because they could not put their hands on the pastor as in time past.

In becoming a mediator, (go between), I had to explain to the department leaders why they had to go to pastor's assistant for some things instead of the pastor.

I had the responsibility of telling old friends of pastor that he wasn't available to them as before. They could no longer go into his office just to get new books he was reading, or just sit and talk..

An old friend of pastor's, who was a pastor himself, would like to browse around in pastor's office and shop. He would take books, bibles, cologne, and pens. With the change in the chain of command established, some of the immediate family and lower level staff members had a hard time dealing with supervisors. What surprises me the most is that if they were working in the secular world, they would have to deal with a chain of command? But in the church, saints have a problem. Members who were pillars of the ministry felt that they had the right to see the pastor anytime they desired. One member told me that since she gives her money to the church, she should be able to come into the office area anytime she wanted.

Family members in ministry. For many personal secretaries, dealing with the leader's family is more stressful than working in the world. One secretary told me that the children were worst in terms of following rules than members. I had the opportunity to sit in on a workshop for pastors who were discussing different issues with their overseer. The dominate discussion was how do they deal with family members. There are family members who feel that they have a right to interrupt meetings, get everything free when others have to pay, and are of the privilege class when their parent, aunt or uncle is the leader of a ministry. They want offices, cars, homes, free lunch or dinner and salaries just because they are a family member. The said thing about it, for the most part many get just what they want. Office administrators are given instruction for members but not to family members. Why aren't some of these children working a regular job? Some not all family members cannot hold a job because they cannot get away with some of this stuff as they get away with in ministry!!

I have witnessed leader's family members that are just plain rude!! It should be up to the leader to handle these situations. But I have found that they do not. Some feel so guilty that they have not spent time with their families that they just give into their children.

A wonderful, faithful woman of God left the ministry I attended, because the daughter of the pastor scolded her in front of other members. This same daughter came against an elder in the ministry for correcting her son. Once a leader tried to correct her daughter during a meeting, and the daughter replied, "why are you saying this to me now, this is not what you say at home?" We just dropped our heads and remained silent. If a family member has anything to do with any part of the worship service, they come late and feel as if the service is centered on them. Now let me be perfectly clear, not every pastor's kid, niece, nephew or grandchild is like this. I have come across some very respectful, caring, God fearing leader's children and family member. They honor God and their parent, however, there are too many that have no respect for anyone. Enough said.

Eventually new people were added to the administrative staff, but their stay was no longer than a few months or weeks. I use to think that it took a special kind of person to work full time in ministry, especially with leaders. Which it does!

I also found out that most people are not willing to put in the amount of time that is required or work for fewer wages than the people at McDonalds received, with no benefits.

It amazes me how some leaders feel that they don't have to pay their employees a fair wage. It is sad how the Word of God is used just to get out of paying a decent salary. Why people stay regardless of what is going on, is because they feel that they are pleasing God. They feel that this is what the Lord would want them to do. I felt the need to stand behind this "code of silence". I felt that I would go to hell if I revealed all that I have seen and witnessed. If you disagreed with your leader, you were coming against God. Proverbs 17:15 states; *"Acquitting the guilty and condemning the innocent - God detests them both."*(NIV)

Do people need to know what is going on in some of these churches? Yes, we need to let the enemy know that he is exposed. No longer will this new generation of the church just sit by and let the devil come in and infiltrate the church as he has for years. Enough is enough!! Let me say this, it is essential that we go to God with all of these issues especially when it comes to leaders. God knows how to take or handle them better than we can.

CHAPTER 19
TV Evangelists

A TV evangelist should **not** be your pastor!! You need to be under a local pastor (shepherd) who has the heart of God. Jeremiah 3:15 clearly states *"And I will give you shepherds after My own heart who shall feed you with knowledge and understanding."* (KJV). Many people who leave the church find themselves staying home and watching the church channels. Staying home and watching 26 minutes of any TV evangelist can make you confused. You really don't know these people. What kind of life are they living. You only see the most exciting parts of their services. Some of the edited parts of the program is what they want you to see in order for you to send them your money. Oh forgive me, so you can become a covenant partner!! Do you know the date these tapes are made and then shown on TV? One TV evangelist said that it's alright to praise dance, another said it's a sin to dance in the church. One TV evangelist said that it's alright to minister in pants another said no. One TV evangelist said it's alright to have homosexuals into your church services another said it is an abomination. One TV evangelist said that it's alright to stomp or listen to crossover music another said "you better not bring that stuff in this church." All of this brings about confusion. Who are you going to listen to? Then who is your covering? Who is watching over your soul? Who can you go to when you need wise counsel? Certainly not a TV evangelist!!! Most of these leaders don't know half of the member's name and certainly not your name. We need leaders to call our name out to the Lord during their time of prayer. Good leaders are watching over our souls. Money is not a major factor, who I am is not a major factor, how I look or even who I know is not a factor to a good leader. But my soul, and if I am in the right standing with God is the major factor. You must be accountable to a leader. If you are sick and cannot attend your local church that is one thing. Even in being home you must go to God on who you should listen to or watch. Perhaps you could purchase DVD's of previous services that you may listen to during your absence. But please don't depend on the TV for your spiritual growth. I know with all that I have revealed to you in this book, you are wondering why would I say such a thing. I really believe and know without a doubt that there are some wonderful, anointed, men and women of God who truly have the heart of the father. Not everyone in the church of our God is a hypocrite and abusive to the body of Christ. And I am keenly aware that there are some things exclusively for God to handle.

But what I have been assigned to do it help someone who has experienced some of what I have shared in this book is to let you know that you are not alone as the enemy would want you to think. God see and he hears all that is going on. It is all about God and His Kingdom. Not in people, but God and Him alone.

CHAPTER 20
Forgiveness

I think the most important point I want you to know is that there is power in forgiveness. With all that has been exposed in this book, the enemy has been identified. Now be delivered, be healed and set free!! Forgive, forgive, and forgive. Love, love, and love. Not our kind of love, but the agape love of God. We must go on to the next dimension in the Lord. We can't go forward, always looking back. I loved my father more than ever before he went home to be with the Lord. He transitioned into a wonderful and powerful man of God. He was not the same man I had known in my younger years and I was not the same as well. My dad left his children with a legacy that we are proud to follow. The last day I spoke with my father, he again asked us to forgive him to make sure it was well and he then blessed all of his children as we stood at the hospital bed. He encouraged us to stay with the Lord and love the Lord with all our heart and soul. He told me that he was proud of me in ministry and wanted me to work with him in Richmond. It was through forgiveness I was able to minister to him and him to me, without hatred in my heart, without anger in my heart, bitterness or indifference. This was the work of the Lord who changed the spirit of my mind, heart and inner emotions. I want the Lord and His fullness more than I wanted to hurt and hold on to damage emotions.

I wanted to learn from God the correct way of raising my children. I want God to teach me how to truly love and honor the gift, my children, which he has given my husband and me. I wanted to hear my children say to their friends "my parents are our role models". But most of all, I want God to be pleased with our home and our lives. My husband and I are closer than ever. Of course we have intense fellowship meetings, we have problems, my children can take me to a level I have not known. Sometimes I just want to pack-up and leave. Let the children have the house!! The members of our church can get on my nerves. But I have learned where to go and how to handle these situations. My husband and I no longer fight over the hours I spend in ministry. Together, we talk, together we pray, together we hold hand and laugh.

I have the privilege of teaching secretaries/administrators they must realize the importance of their role in ministry. But they must also know that they must answer to God for all that they do.

God places us in a particular ministry to be a help. But in being a help don't find yourselves dying a silent spiritual death. We must maintain a firm, solid relationship with the Lord.

In my younger years I used to ask the Lord, "Lord why have you allowed me to go through abuse, see and hear so much in ministry"? Now I know why. To help those who are experiencing the same things in this day and time. To let them know that they are not alone. There are so many people who will not talk about the abuse and injustice they have experienced. But they will pick up a book and read it in the privacy of their homes.

Old things must pass away, all things will become new. It is a new time, a new freedom, a new day to enjoy the God of our salvation. God is even rising up new leaders. He is bringing them to the forefront. People we have never heard of before are now coming forth with power, integrity and the very nature of Christ. This is the remnant of God. Are you part of the remnant?

To those who are hurting in any way, don't give up. Don't stop praying. Continue to seek the Lord. I found out that God is a heart healer as well as a physical healer. After I was hurt in the church, the devil tried to get me to stay home and feel sorry for myself. I almost secluded myself in my home. But the devil must have forgotten the relationship I had with the Lord previously.

When I was home for a period of time, I was fasting, praying, crying and writing this book. There were times, I had to look in the mirror and encourage myself. Different ones would come to visit me to question me as to why we left the former church I was in. They left our home only with the Word of the Lord and scriptures to read on what God has to say about being a busy body.

I told you it is a new day and new time. We don't have time for gossip and slander. We must do the work of the Lord my demonstrating the nature and character of our Lord and Savior Jesus Christ. Our Redeemer is coming back real soon. He is coming back Sooner than we can even imagine. There are too many people who are trying to capture the minds of our children, while the devil is trying to discourage, and put weights on the parents. The enemy wants to "frustrate" the people of God.

Let those who refuse to renew their mind continue to bicker among themselves. While they are bickering over dress, seats, which said what, hairstyles, should one listen to traditional gospel or contemporary gospel, and who has the closest relationship with the pastor, God is rising up a group of people who could care less about such things. All they care about is honoring and loving the Lord. Their outlook is if you would truly seek the Lord, He has all the answers.

In this edition of this book the Lord has impressed upon me to illuminate so much of what I had previously written. Some of which will be in my next book.

Finally, let's break the Code of Silence in the church. If the enemy can keep us silent there will not be any deliverance for others. It's our speaking out that let others know that they are not alone. God can deliver you from hurt, abuse, and misuse and help you forgive the abusers.

Pray for us as we go before the Lord for our next book.

Prayer:

Father, in the Precious name of Jesus, we thank you for Who you are to us. Only You are our lifeline, only You are our Redeemer and only You have forgiven us of our sins and have washed us clean with Your Precious Blood.

I thank you Father for all that you have done and are doing for your church. You are bringing us back to the reality of Your Word and what you have called Your church to be in the earth.

Forgive us for the abuse, misuse, mishandling, judging, and ostracizing your people and rebelling against all that you have placed in our hands to do. Wash us with hyssop that we may be clean and pure before you a Holy and Righteous God.

Bless your leaders and help them everywhere to hear you correctly and obey You so that they may leader your people as You have appointed and called them to do. I ask you Lord that you make their thoughts agreeable to Your will so your vision that You have given are established and will succeed.

For you have declared just as Your servant Moses followed Your specific instruction in building Your tabernacle, so must we follow Your instructions so that You may dwell among Your people. There is a remnant that is seeking after You. There is a remnant that is crying out to You. There is a remnant that love and will obey You, God.

I pray that you God help us, everywhere, not to remain selfish, bitter and unforgiving, for if we obey You and follow You, there will not be any hard place. It is only in you there are no struggles. For we are well aware to whom we must answer too and whom we serve. I pray that you Lord, help us to maintain your character and nature at all times.

We have the right and authority by You God to decree and declare abundant blessing of You, to rest upon all who reads this book. Take us to the place, the secret place in You that we may dwell with you. We praise only You and we worship only You Father. We thank you Father for your son, Jesus. Jesus we thank you for your blood. The blood that purifies delivers and is powerful. We thank you Holy Spirit. For you are the Spirit which came down to from heaven to lead and guide us as the Father has instructed. We thank you Father for hearing us and answering our prayer. All this in the powerful and wonderful name of our Lord and Savior Jesus the Christ.

Chapter 20

CPSIA information can be obtained at www.ICGtesting.com
Printed in the USA
BVOW06s1428170216

437074BV00008B/15/P

9 780991 424658